LIBRARY

for

by

DISTRIBUTED BY THE

GUIDE

BRAZILIAN STUDIES

WILLIAM VERNON JACKSON

PITTSBURGH   •   1964

UNIVERSITY OF PITTSBURGH BOOK CENTERS

Art Work by Douglas M. Hieber
Maps by James A. Bier

PHOTOLITHOPRINTED BY CUSHING - MALLOY, INC.
ANN ARBOR, MICHIGAN, UNITED STATES OF AMERICA
1964

♦ to L.D.J.
and W.O.J.

 Preface

For some time the lack of adequate guides to American library resources for Latin American studies has handicapped students and scholars interested in this area. The decision to focus the Eighth Seminar on the Acquisition of Latin American Library Materials (SALALM) on bibliographical and library matters relating to Brazil stimulated the preparation of this work. Although all data collected in the spring of 1963 could not be made available for the meeting of the Seminar, held at the University of Wisconsin in July, a preliminary version of this study, with the title "American Library Resources for Brazilian Studies," appeared as one of the working papers.

During the following year it was possible not only to obtain coverage of additional libraries, but also to prepare the union list of Brazilian periodicals (Appendix 2) and the index to Brazil in the Library of Congress Classification (Appendix 5).

This survey describes the state of holdings in 1963 and 1964. Because information did not come from all libraries at the same time, the resources of some institutions reflect anywhere from several months to a year's more acquisitions than those of other collections. In general, the final date for inclusion of material was July 1964.

Since the purpose of this study was to present materials useful for advanced study and research, it deals, with some exceptions, only with holdings of the country's major research collections. No attempt was made to include information on college, special, and public libraries, which presumably have only limited resources for Brazilian studies. Without the cooperation of the seventy-four libraries listed in Appendix 1, this Guide could not have been prepared, and I am most grateful to them for all the information which they supplied.

The Grants Committee of the Association of College and Research Libraries acceded to a request for funds to visit selected institutions, and appointment as a consultant to the Hispanic Foundation, Library of Congress, permitted a more extensive survey of the national library's collections than would otherwise have been possible. A University of Wisconsin faculty research grant also provided assistance for the preparation of this Guide.

Special thanks go to Irene Zimmerman for permission to include in the union list (Appendix 2) extracts from her annotations of Brazilian periodicals. I also appreciate the suggestions made by a number of colleagues who read over the preliminary version of the study, a great deal of assistance of various kinds that Donald K. Lamb cheerfully provided, and the special typing that Judith Govan Nauman did. Janet Phillips prepared the manuscript for publication with her usual competence.

W. V. J.

Park Ridge, Illinois
September 10, 1964

Table of Contents

List of Tables and Maps

 Introduction

Over twenty years ago Stefan Zweig characterized Brazil as the land of the future. This nation, largest and most populous in Latin America, has aroused the interest of more and more Americans in recent years, as it has moved from an underdeveloped country toward an industrialized society. Recently the Alliance for Progress has stimulated further awareness of Latin America in general and of individual countries in particular. It is not surprising then to find that the increasing attention Brazil is receiving from universities and foundations, government and business has in turn brought about a growing concern for adequate library resources to support their programs and activities. This raises a number of questions: Which American libraries have collected materials needed for advanced study and research on Brazil? How extensively have they done so? In which subjects are these collections strong? In which areas are they weak?

The search for answers to these questions resulted in this guide, which has the following objectives:

1. To indicate which libraries are the major repositories of material about Brazil (and conversely those institutions which at the present time have relatively less important holdings)
2. To describe and evaluate resources available for all important subject areas, to show where strength lies and to point out weakness
3. To assist students, scholars, and others interested in Brazil to find the best material in their fields, particularly by indicating which materials may be available close at hand
4. To show which libraries are acquiring current Brazilian publications
5. To provide specific information on the holdings available

in this country of nearly one hundred significant Brazilian journals in the humanities and social sciences
6. To offer a key to the place of material on Brazil in the Library of Congress Classification, a scheme increasingly used not only in large libraries but also in bibliographic activities
7. To provide a basis for closer cooperation among libraries that specialize in Brazilian materials, so that resources may be improved on a national basis and unnecessary duplication avoided

It does not attempt to trace the history of collections (fascinating as that might be), nor to discuss their organization, administration, and finance. On the other hand, in cases where libraries have stated their acquisition policies, such information has been incorporated into the appropriate descriptions of resources.

EXISTING GUIDES TO RESOURCES

The person interested in Brazil might expect to find a great deal of information in the surveys of resources, library guides and handbooks, union lists, and the like, that have appeared in the past twenty-five years, but the standard tools of this kind prove to be disappointing in the amount of help they provide.

The survey of leading collections made in 1942 (23)* mentions Brazil only under Latin American history and does not provide a separate tabulation for Portuguese language and literature, although for a number of subjects (e.g., folklore, fine arts, geography, anthropology, and ethnology) there is reference to Latin America without specific indication of Brazil. More recently Ash's compilation (2) has three entries under "Brazil" and one each under "Brazil--History," "Brazil--Social Life and Customs" and "Brazilian Language and Literature." To the person interested in the over-all picture this is less helpful than it appears, because four of the six entries refer to the same library, as does the single listing in the 1963 Directory of Special Libraries and Information Centers (42). However, the Index to Special Collections in the Union Catalog Division of the Library of Congress records thirteen libraries with collections on Brazil.

More useful than any of these, however, in terms of providing specific information is Hilton's Handbook of Hispanic Source Materials (34), although for most institutions its coverage of library resources is brief.

---

* Numbers in parentheses refer to items in the Bibliography, beginning on page 83.

The person consulting Downs's bibliography and its supplement* finds six references under "Brazil" in the index (entries under "Latin America" suggest possible additional sources of information).

There are several reasons why all of this literature fails to provide an adequate picture of resources for Brazilian studies in American research libraries. In the first place, much of it appeared so many years ago as to be out-of-date or inaccurate--e.g., at one institution plans to develop a Brazilian collection never did materialize. With few exceptions the publications mentioned above are enumerative rather than descriptive. Moreover, the concept of area studies with an inter-disciplinary approach is a relatively new one, and consequently is not adequately reflected in older bibliographical publications, which tend to describe resources in one discipline for all of Latin America rather than resources in various fields for study of a single country. The incompleteness of the picture calls for a fresh approach, if we are to know what resources for advanced study and research on Brazil are available in the United States.

METHODOLOGY OF THE PRESENT STUDY

In spite of these limitations in available surveys the first step in preparing the present study consisted of a thorough review of the existing literature of library resources. Because titles are misleading and indexing often fails to bring out the country approach, it was necessary to examine carefully the major national, regional, and local guides, descriptions of holdings of individual libraries and those of special collections in the Latin American field, as well as bibliographies which might supply locations for the items listed. No attempt was made, however, to scan all regional and local union lists of serials. Even after discarding many titles which, although in some cases indicating strength in Latin American holdings, proved not to make specific mention of Brazil, this yielded a total of 125 items (listed in the Bibliography) that deal in whole or in part with resources for Brazilian studies in the United States. Such a literature search obviously reveals the holdings of libraries only to the extent that they have been active in publishing, and many major institutions have done little to describe their resources. Moreover, many checklists, such as those appearing in the _Bulletin_ of the New York Public Library and the Bibliographic Series of the Pan American Union, reveal

---

* Robert B. Downs, _American Library Resources, A Bibliographical Guide_ and _Supplement_ (Chicago, American Library Association, 1951 and 1962).

the state of collections as they were anywhere from a few years to a half century ago.

For this reason, assistance from libraries themselves was sought; a letter sent to members of the Association of Research Libraries (and a few other institutions) requested information about their total resources on Brazil (i.e., general items and material in the various disciplines of the humanities, social sciences, and science and technology). Because serial holdings have assumed such importance as the medium for dissemination of research, the circular also asked for holdings of the ninety-eight periodicals appearing in the Zimmerman list.* Although this yielded a large quantity of information, the data furnished varied greatly in accordance with the interpretation placed on the request by libraries and with the amount of time they found it possible to devote to preparing replies.

Personal investigation constituted a third method utilized in making this study. While very effective in achieving uniformity of coverage, it was also the most time consuming. Any attempt to visit all, or even a majority, of the principal research libraries would have delayed unduly the completion of this work. Fortunately the extensive holdings of the Library of Congress were investigated in this fashion as well as through printed sources.

It was not possible to apply a fourth technique--utilizing checklists--for more than two samples, one list of histories of literature and one of nineteenth century travel books, but in each case holdings were obtained from the National Union Catalog.

This survey of American library resources for Brazilian studies draws on the information accumulated through all four techniques. Even so, it cannot pretend to be comprehensive or even uniform in its coverage. Holdings of Library A figure more prominently in subject X than those of Library B, because for one reason or another more material suitable for incorporation was available, even though in fact Library B's resources may be equally good. Moreover, smaller institutions often reported as significant holdings what would be taken for granted in large collections like Harvard, the New York Public, and the Library of Congress. It is hoped, however, that omissions of notable resources have been few and that this survey at least guides the reader to holdings useful to him.

---

*Irene Zimmerman, *A Guide to Current Latin American Periodicals: Humanities and Social Sciences* (Gainesville, Fla., Kallman Publishing Co., 1961).

ORGANIZATION

Of the several possible ways to arrange information on library resources it appeared that the most useful one might be to follow the usual academic disciplines. There are thus chapters covering the humanities, the social sciences, and science and technology. Preceding them come sections on general bibliographical materials and on such special forms as manuscripts, archival materials, government publications, general periodicals, and newspapers (periodical resources for the most part are treated with monographic holdings on the same subject and maps in the section on geography). In some cases it was necessary to make arbitrary decisions, because library classification does not always follow academic fields, and some institutions found it convenient to report in terms of their classification (Dewey Decimal or Library of Congress).

Since the aim of the resources survey is to describe collections rather than to list individual works, the account which follows provides, insofar as possible, information on the extent of holdings, special features and emphases, mention of strengths and weaknesses and (where appropriate) of periods covered, geographical range, and language spread; given the large size of Brazil, special effort is made to indicate emphasis on a particular region, state, or city whenever it exists. Specific titles are of course omitted, except when outstanding or valuable or when cited as representative examples. The reader must bear in mind that designations like strong and weak are subjective and relative and that quantitative and qualitative comparisons between collections should be made with caution. Comments on periodical holdings follow the descriptive section for each discipline; because full information appears in the union list (Appendix 2), it seems unnecessary to do more than to point out the extent and distribution of complete--or best available--files.

Three additional appendices will, it is hoped, prove useful to the reader. The first two present the Library of Congress Classification for Brazilian history and description (from Class F) and for Brazilian literature (from Class PQ). The third offers an extensive, if not comprehensive, index to materials on Brazil in the Library of Congress Classification, as an aid to the person seeking to locate works on specific topics in a library or bibliography which utilizes that scheme.

General
Materials

2

The number of research libraries in the United States depends on one's definition of research library, but few persons doubt that at least seventy-five institutions--most of them universities--possess significant resources from the national point of view. Since development of holdings has varied from one library to another, the number of strong collections available for any given subject field is considerably less than this total; it is even more difficult to determine how many strong collections may exist on a given area like Latin America or even on a specific country like Brazil.

Seventy-four libraries* supplied information about their holdings for use in this study. Since a number of them, including American Antiquarian, Boston University, Cincinnati, Connecticut, Emory, Florida State, Georgia Institute of Technology, Iowa State University of Science and Technology, 'Maryland, Massachusetts Institute of Technology, Midwest Inter-Library Center, New York State, Oklahoma State, Pennsylvania State, Pittsburgh, Rochester, St. Louis, Southern California, Tennessee, Utah, Washington State, Washington (St. Louis), and Wayne State, indicate that at this time they do not collect material for Brazilian studies to any significan degree or have only recently embarked upon a program of Brazilian acquisitions, they receive but little mention in this survey. Five other institutions--Boston Public, Johns Hopkins, Nebraska, Notre Dame, and Oregon--are represented in the union list of periodicals (Appendix 2), because they

---

* See Appendix I for a list. Since the names of these libraries appear in full there, they are identified in the text by short forms (e.g., Harvard, Oklahoma State, Cleveland Public) except where confusion might result (e.g., New York Public and New York University).

have supplied information only about their holdings of the ninety-eight titles on the circular. In some cases large libraries report that they are making no effort to develop more than working collections. This then leaves two groups of institutions whose resources are especially important--the very large general collections (e.g., Harvard, Library of Congress, New York Public) which on the basis of their total resources alone hold considerable quantities of Brazilian material and others (e.g., Florida, Joint University Libraries, Pan American Union) which have, for one reason or another, developed significant holdings of Braziliana.

In addition, there are four special collections--used here in the sense of identifiable units (at least at the time of acquisition)--devoted in whole or in large part to Brazil. Since the following pages contain many references to their holdings in specific subject areas, it may be useful to note at this point the general nature of each.

The John Casper Branner Collection at Stanford (34) contained 6,000 items when received. Strong in Brazilian history, it also includes scholarly books of travel dealing with economic, political, and social conditions, flora and fauna, anthropology and ethnology. There are government publications and files of journals.

Cornell acquired the Francis Reginald Hull Collection of 4,000 volumes (34, 87) in 1948. It covers political history and cultural development in Brazil, the Brazilian economy over the centuries and also provides general historical and cultural background for South America.

The William B. Greenlee Collection at Newberry Library (7,67,89) centers on the history and literature of Portugal, in which Brazil figures as a Portuguese colony. Thus holdings, while covering Brazil's political, religious, social, cultural, and economic development, stress the colonial period.

Fourth of the special collections, the Oliveira Lima Library at Catholic University of America (14,22,42,54,88) specializes in Luso-Brazilian history and civilization. (It also includes more limited resources on Spain and Spanish American language, literature and history.) Holdings on Brazil emphasize history, language and literature, travel, and church history. There are many government documents, publications of Brazilian archives and journal files, as well as reference and bibliographical material. Resources now amount to approximately 45,000 volumes.

MANUSCRIPTS

Even with the appearance of the first two volumes of The National Union Catalog of Manuscript Collections (62), it is probable that only a small portion of the manuscripts in this country dealing with Brazil have been listed; such items tend to be found within larger collections rather than existing as separate manuscript groups.   The following recapitulation covers items appearing in the first two volumes; it is followed by some indication of the holdings of selected major repositories.

It is not surprising to find that a significant number of manuscripts deal with political and diplomatic history.   For instance, in the letters of Henry Clay, written while he was Secretary of State and now at the Henry E. Huntington Library, there are references to the independence of Brazil and to possibilities of commerce with her.   In the Historical Society of Pennsylvania are two volumes of letters from Condy Raguet (1784-1842), U.S. chargé d'affaires at the Court of Brazil, to John Quincy Adams and Henry Clay, Secretaries of State, concerning relations with the Brazilian government, commercial and shipping conditions, revolutionary developments, and other subjects.

Two sets of papers provide information about southern families who left the United States after the Civil War.   The Keyes family papers in the University of Alabama Library concern the emigration of the family of John Washington Keyes to Rio de Janeiro.   There are accounts by his wife called "Our Life in Brazil," and the Brazilian letters span the period 1867-1935.   The Barnsley family papers in Duke University contain letters from George and Lucien Barnsley, who joined an ex-Confederate group which migrated to South America; they describe the natives, the countryside, and political, social, and economic conditions in the Sao Paulo and Rio de Janeiro area.   The papers of James Monroe (1821-1898), U.S. consul in Rio de Janeiro from 1863 to 1870, might shed further light on the immigration of such families; they are located in the Oberlin College Library.

At the University of Virginia, in the papers of Richard Harding Davis (1864-1916), are correspondence, clippings, tracts, etc. (1907-1909) relative to Sebastian H. L. de Magali's Brazil filibuster incident.

Travel literature also bulks large.   There are papers of William Clay Cumming with a few comments on his visit in 1816 to Brazil and Uruguay (in Duke); journals of Charles Crillon Barton (d. 1851) written during a cruise on the U.S.S. Hornet to

the West Indies (1827) and off the coast of Brazil on the U.S.S.
Vandalia and U.S.S. Hudson (1828-1831) and notes of Commodore
Samuel Woodhouse on a tour of Brazil in 1818 (in the Historical
Society of Pennsylvania); correspondence, the logbook, and order
book of the U.S.S. Wyoming concerning a voyage from Philadelphia to Honolulu (1859-1861) with visits at Rio de Janeiro and
other cities (in Virginia Historical Society); letters of Samuel
William Weston describing a trip to Brazil (in Mississippi Department of Archives) and a notebook kept in 1870 by William
Stebbins Barnard (1875-1947) during a journey to Brazil (in Cornell).   The papers of President Theodore Roosevelt in the University of Virginia Library contain the carbon copy of "Through
the Brazilian Hinterland" (published in 1914 as Through the
Brazilian Wilderness), together with letters of transmittal and
twelve leaves of the original manuscript version.

Another important group of manuscripts deal with trade,
commerce, and transportation.   Letters from Ebeneezer Francis
Osborne (in Cornell) describe a voyage (1825-1828) as supercargo
to Rio de Janeiro and other South American cities, while the
letter book of Samuel A. Fabens (1812-1899) contains letters and
sailing orders on his voyages in the ship Ariosto to Rio de Janeiro
and other ports (in the Essex Institute) and that of B.H. Devereux,
a merchant and shipper of Pernambuco, preserves correspondence
to his clients in the United States concerning his commercial enterprises in sugar, coffee, and other commodities (in Historical
Society of Pennsylvania).   The papers of David Bullock Harris
(1814-1864), a tobacco exporter and Confederate officer of Louisa
County, Virginia, relate to his tobacco business and Brazilian
commerce with this country (in Duke).   Letters on efforts to obtain from the Brazilian government a monopoly of steam navigation on the Amazon River, along with descriptive comments on
the country and its politics, are found in the papers of Peter A.
Remsen (1786-1852) (in State Historical Society of Wisconsin).
Two groups of papers in the University of Oregon relate to trans-
portion: those of Thomas Osmonde Russell (1881-1961) embrace
correspondence, designs and plans relating to the Itabira Railroad planned for the Companhia Itabira do Brasil and those of
Clyde Bruce Aitchison (1875-1962), Interstate Commerce Commissioner, have documents and correspondence on the regulation
of transportation in Brazil.

Southern Baptist Theological Seminary in Louisville has
nine volumes of manuscripts relating to Baptist missions from
1854 to 1953.   They include Baptist beginnings in the Amazon
valley region and northern Brazil, together with "Years on the
Amazon, 1891-1939" by Enrico A. Nelson.   In Concordia Histor-

ical Institute, St. Louis, copies of letters of Heinrich Christian
Schwan (1819-1905) to his parents describe Bahia and Schwan's
work there as a Lutheran clergyman and church official.

The Henry E. Huntington Library has the papers of John
Casper Branner (1850-1922), geologist and president of Stanford
University. There are about one hundred items: diaries, field
notes, material for an autobiography, scientific data on Brazil,
and other papers. The University of West Virginia contains correspondence and notes on the activities of Israel Charles White
(1848-1927) as chief of the Brazilian Coal Commission, 1904-1906.

Turning now to several libraries with large manuscript
collections, one observes that the lack of a guide to the holdings
of Library of Congress makes it impossible to know with certain-
ty the extent of its holdings. However, there are three groups relating to the Dutch West India Co.; one contains copies of its accounts, resolutions, and reports, nearly all from the period
1645-1650; another consists of copies of reports dealing with the
Company's activities in Brazil, 1636-1644; and the third is apparently the Company's volume of the resolutions of the Staten
Generaal on commerce with Brazil. There is a four-volume
manuscript entitled "Chrónicas Lageanas or A Record of Facts
and Observations on Manners and Customs in South Brazil Ex-
tracted from Notes Taken on the Spot, During a Period of More
than Twenty Years," by R. Cleary , covering the history, geography, and social condition of Lages from 1685 to 1885. A shorter work by Cleary appears to be an abridgment of the "Chrónicas"
and bears the title "Brazil Under the Monarchy, A Record of
Facts and Observations from Notes Taken in Brazil During a
Period of More than Twenty Years [1865-1889?]. "

Of more recent date are the minutes of each meeting of the
directors of the Recife and São Francisco Pernambuco Railway
Co., authenticated by signatures of the secretary or chairman,
dated Oct. 11, 1854-Nov. 11, 1856 and Aug.4, 1857-June 21, 1861.
The papers of Frank Lamson-Scribner (1851-1938) include material on exhibits he helped prepare for the Exposição do Centenário
do Brasil, 1922-1923, and those of Breckinridge Long (1881-1958)
items on his career as Third Assistant Secretary of State under
Woodrow Wilson (1917-1920), Ambassador on a special mission
to Brazil, Argentina, and Uruguay (1938) and as Assistant Secretary of State under Franklin Delano Roosevelt (1940-1944).

In the material known as the Portuguese Manuscript Collection (105-c), acquired by the library in 1928 and consisting of
items collected by Conde dos Olivaes e de Penha Longa and by

Antônio Augusto de Carvalho Monteiro, are an estimated seventy items dealing with Brazil. Examples of the more interesting and important are (a) the notebooks, correspondence, notes and bills of Rudolph Waehneldt covering the mid-nineteenth century; (b) the diary and notes of Luiz Antonio Alves Carvalho--most of the entries written in Rio and Petropolis in 1874 and 1875; (c) items from the Carvalho Monteiro collection of Camoniana pertaining to Camões and the Lusíadas in Brazil; (d) Register of letters written by Manoel da Cunha Menezes in Bahia, 1774-1779, concerning Brazilian affairs along the southern frontier, appointment of officers and garrisoning of fortifications, conflicts between military and regular orders and royal and other authority and (e) Military Orders, 1706-1799, largely copies of consultas, petições, decrees, and letters from the records of the Mesa de Consciencia e Ordens.

The Manuel E. Gondra Collection at Texas (13, 101) consists to a large extent of copies made in long hand or by typewriter from the originals found in the Archivo de las Indias in Seville, the archives of Simancas, the British Museum, and the Archivo Nacional of Paraguay. A few originals are mostly of the nineteenth and twentieth centuries. Here one finds numerous reports and petitions, ranging in time from 1638 to the nineteenth century, relating to the incursions of the Portuguese of Brazil into Paraguay. The collection amounts to several hundred folios.

There are two relevant collections in the University's Texas Archives (62): the papers of Mary Decherd contain correspondence with missionaries in Brazil and with various other Methodists, mostly relating to the mission established in Passo Fundo by Methodist students of the University of Texas, as well as progress reports, checks, receipts, statements, news clippings, other printed material, and photographs relating to this mission. Correspondence with mathematicians in Brazil and other countries is found in the letters of Edward Lewis Dodd (1875-1943).

Harvard (40) has a number of manuscripts relating to Brazil. The journals of William Dane Phelps (1802-1875) include a notebook on Brazil and the Mediterranean, 1828-1833; others are a captain's logbook for 1861; orders of the day for the Brazilian Army during the Paraguayan War; a translation of Vicente Alves de Paula Pessoa entitled "A Brief History of Brazil"; log of the Isaac Ellis, New York to Rio de Janiero and return, 1837-1838; an autograph letter signed of Emperor Pedro II; and items relating to the Brazil Railway Co., 1914-1920, among the business papers of W. Cameron Forbes in the Baker Library of the Business School (the journals of Forbes, in the Manuscript Division of Library of Congress, contain additional information on the railway).

The New York Public (53) reports that its manuscripts include papers dealing with Brazil in the Rich Collection; material
by individual authors (e.g., Machado de Assis); and eighteen
letters and documents of the Dutch West India Company relating
to Brazil, 1624-1670; but that perhaps the most important item,
consisting of twenty-six volumes, is "Brazil. Collecçao authen-
tica de todas as Leys, Regimentos, Alvaras, e mais ordens, que
se expediram para o Brazil desde o estabelecimento destas Con-
quistas. Ordenada por Provizam de 28 de Março de 1754."

In the Oliveira Lima Library at Catholic   University of
America (12, 71) are numerous manuscripts. They consist of
three groups: the bound or collected documents; a number of letters originally in the possession of João Artur de Sousa Correia
(d. 1900); and miscellaneous papers. The first two groups deal
more with Portugal than with Brazil, but the third is composed
mainly of Brazilian letters written in the nineteenth century on a
variety of commercial, religious, educational, and governmental
affairs. In addition, the Library contains the Oliveira Lima
family papers (1884-1926), which occupy five file cabinets; the
research collection of Manoel de Oliveira Lima, together with
more than sixty scrapbooks filled with newspaper clippings and
memorabilia; and Brazilian diplomatic papers from the legation
in Brussels (1908-1914).

ARCHIVAL MATERIALS

The National Archives contain a significant amount of material relating to Brazil (30, 31, 56, 121-123). Probably of greatest interest are the non-current diplomatic and consular post
archives; these embrace ninety-five per cent of the post records
prior to 1935. Material from the Brazilian diplomatic post--like
that from Mexico, Cuba, and Panama--is considerably more extensive than that from Argentina and other Latin American countries; it spans the period from 1809 to 1935 and consists of seventy-nine cubic feet of instructions from the Department of State,
and copies of duplicates of despatches to it; notes from the government of Brazil, and copies of notes to it; copies of instructions and communications to subordinate consulates, and despatches and reports from them; miscellaneous correspondence received and sent; records of passports issued and visaed; records of
births, marriages, and deaths of American citizens; records concerning the disposal of property, the settlement of estates, and
the protection of American citizens; journals of events and memo-
randa; and financial records and property inventories of the posts.
Records and indexes are present, and the bulk of the material

consists of bound volumes.

Brazilian consular posts represented and the extent of material available for each appear in Table I. This material is in many ways similar to that found in the archives of diplomatic posts; the description of records from Bahia may serve as a specific illustration of what is generally available. Some of the more interesting types of information are as follows. The Fee Books contain, in addition to information on fees collected for certification of crew lists and cargoes and authentication of marine notes of protest, information on desertions and deaths among the crew, deviations from voyage, sale of cargoes, and dates of arrival and clearance. The Miscellaneous Record Book has letters from and copies of letters to provincial officials, remarks on the visits of the Boston Chamber of Commerce and President Theodore Roosevelt. There are press copies of despatches to the Department of State, miscellaneous letters received from government agencies in the United States, naval officers in Brazilian waters, other American consulates and the legation in Rio de Janeiro. The 138 volumes of Correspondence (1913-1935) embrace the originals of all incoming correspondence, with enclosures, and typed carbons of all outgoing correspondence, with duplicates of enclosures; the correspondence--chiefly with American business firms and private individuals, officials of the Department of State and other government agencies--deals mainly with commerce and commercial relations and internal affairs of state. There are various records which provide a fairly detailed statistical account of American shipping activities in Bahia; a register book records births, deaths, marriages, and citizenship papers involving Americans.

Archives of the posts at Belém, Manaus, and Iquitos provide source material on the building of the Madeira-Mamoré Railroad and such aspects of the rubber industry in the Amazon basin as finance, transportation, and labor relations.

It should be remembered that the year 1912 marks a major difference in the organization of post archives. Prior to that date the records were kept in several series of volumes, each devoted to a particular type of record--e.g., fee books, records of arrivals and departures of American vessels and instructions from the Department of State. After 1912 a single series of volumes contains all of the correspondence and most other post records. Within each calendar year the arrangement is by subject classification (the nine main classes are miscellaneous; U.S. government administration; extradition; protection of interests; claims; international congresses, conferences and treaties; commerce and com-

TABLE I

RECORDS OF BRAZILIAN CONSULAR POSTS
IN THE NATIONAL ARCHIVES

Post	Period Covered	Extent *
Aracaju	1883 - 1905	1 ft.
Belém	1831 - 1939	36 ft. **
Belo Horizonte	1942 - 1946	7 ft.
Ceará	1849 - 1934	3 ft.
Florianópolis	1940 - 1944	2 ft.
Maceió	1890 - 1913	1 vol.
Manáos***	1882 - 1928; 1941 - 1946	20 ft.
Maranhão	1852 - 1925	5 ft.
Natal	1880 - 1947	13 ft.
Pernambuco (Recife)	1818 - 1936	63 ft.
Pôrto Alegre	1917 - 1941	23 ft.
Rio de Janeiro	1833 - 1936	130 ft.
Rio Grande	1829 - 1911; 1913 - 1940	17 ft.
Salvador (Bahia)	1819 - 1935	65 ft.
Santa Catarina	1833 - 1874	5 vols.
Santos	1880 - 1935	34 ft.
São Paulo	1907 - 1935	36 ft.
Vitória	1890 - 1932	7 ft.

*Footages indicated are cubic
**Including records from Manáos
***See also Belém

SOURCE: Derived from U.S. National Archives. List of Foreign
Service Post Records in the National Archives, pp. 9-28.

mercial relations; relations of state; and internal affairs of state);
under each subject the arrangement is first by particular case
and then chronologically.

The applications and recommendations for office in the Department of State, 1791-1901, consist of letters from successful
and unsuccessful applicants for office, letters and petitions supporting their appointments and letters either opposing the appli-
cant or complaining of his actions after he was appointed. The
series covering diplomatic representatives of the United States to
Brazil contains items relating to the following: Condy Raguet,

1817-1825; William Tudor, 1809-1817; William Hunter, 1829-1836;
Robert C. Schenck, 1845-1852; William Trousdale, 1853-1861;
Richard Kidder Meade, 1853-1861; James Watson Webb, 1845-
1852 and 1861-1869; Henry T. Blow, 1861-1869; Joseph R. Part-
ridge, 1861-1869; Henry W. Hilliard, 1869-1885; Thomas A.
Osborn, 1877-1885; Thomas J. Jarvis, 1885-1893; Robert Adams,
Jr., 1885-1893; Thomas L. Thompson, 1893-1897; and Edwin H.
Conger, 1897-1901.

There are the records of claims against Brazil under the
convention of 1849, most of them dealing with complaints of
United States commercial and whaling interests that their property
had been illegally taxed or confiscated during the 1820's and 1830's.
In the records of participation in foreign boundary disputes are
the arguments presented, 1889-1894, by Argentina and Brazil on
the Misiones Territory to the arbitrator, President Grover
Cleveland.

A considerable amount of material in the National Archives
relates to agriculture in Brazil. Dr. James Morrow of the Agricultural Section of the Patent Office visited Rio de Janeiro in
April 1853. In his journal (kept in connection with the expedition
to Japan under Commodore Matthew C. Perry) he describes the
city and its markets and relates what he was able to learn about
Brazilian agriculture. Files of the Office of Foreign Agricultural
Relations of the Department of Agriculture (1911-1940) deal with
the following: trade, cotton, cotton exports, livestock, sugar and
molasses, cocoa, rubber, crop conditions, tobacco, fruit, publications, crop reports, dairy industry, beverages, vegetables,
honey, import policies, international agreements, labor, land
policies, legislation, marketing policies, nuts, oil and oil seeds,
storage, poultry and eggs, prices, production policies, seeds,
silks, spices, textiles, transportation and shipping, wool, agricultural policy, breadstuffs, cooperation, food canning, food-
stuffs, standards, hides and skins, export policies, fibers, feed-
stuffs, and fertilizers. In the correspondence files of the Office
of the Secretary of Agriculture (1879-1933) there are several
hundred items pertaining to Brazil and dealing not only with
Brazilian agriculture, but also trade between the two countries
and introduction of plants from one country to another. The records of the Federal Farm Board include papers relating to the
1931 agreement between the Grain Stabilization Corporation and
the Brazilian government for the barter of 25,000,000 bushels of
wheat for 1,050,000 bags of coffee.

Files of the U.S. Shipping Board Emergency Fleet Corporation provide information about trade and shipping with Brazil,

1920-1936, including vessel operation, repairs, port facilities, fuel oil and coal supplies, labor conditions, and steamship and trading companies. Other agencies represented are the Bureau of Insular Affairs (1898-1934), Joint Information Board on Minerals and Their Derivates (1918), Coast and Geodetic Survey (1906-1932), Bureau of the Mint (1897-1932), and United States Food Administration (1917-1918).

Records of the United States Navy's Brazil Squadron (1841-1861) and South Atlantic Squadron (1865-1885) provide information on the participation of United States vessels in the Brazilian slave trade, the threatened Brazilian attack on Uruguay by land and sea in 1851-1852, the Paraguayan War; they contain lists of United States merchant vessels in Rio de Janeiro and other Brazilian ports. However, for the period 1870-1885 the correspondence is mainly routine. Other records of the Navy and War Departments deal with such topics as war matériel, training of Brazilian officers in the United States, reports by naval attachés and intelligence officers (1910-1932) and activities of the Navy in cooperating with the development of its Brazilian counterpart.

California (Berkeley) has a microfilm collection on colonial Brazil (concentrated between the late sixteenth and early eighteenth centuries) (18). It consists of film made from ninety-five boxes of unbound and 115 boxes of bound materials found in the following Portuguese repositories: Biblioteca da Ajuda, Biblioteca Pública (Oporto), Arquivo Histórico Ultramarino, Arquivo Nacional and Conselho Ultramarino.

GOVERNMENT PUBLICATIONS

The List of Serial Publications of Foreign Governments (44) records the holdings of a number of libraries, but it is now over thirty years old. In general, it shows far greater strength for publications of the Brazilian federal government than for those of the individual states. For items issued by the former there may be ten to twenty locations, while for those issued by the latter often only one or two. Moreover, the collections of federal documents have far fewer lacunae. The preparation of a current list of holdings of Brazilian official publications in American libraries, now underway at the University of Florida, will not only record new publications but will also show the great increase in holdings that has taken place since 1931.

Among major sets of Brazilian congressional documents are those at Library of Congress, New York Public, and Stanford,

each of which possesses substantial runs of the Annaes of the
Câmara dos Deputados and of the Senado. The set in the Oliveira
Lima Library is virtually complete for the imperial period. Stanford also has long runs of the Câmara's Estado de sitio and Inter-
venção nos estados.

Although few libraries mention specifically census and other
statistical publications, it is likely that they are widely distributed,
at least for recent years. Wisconsin's holdings, which begin with
the 1920 census, are probably representative. However, Library
of Congress (112-a, 113) contains a more comprehensive collection, including a complete set of the twenty-two volumes of the
first census, Recenseamento de população do Império de Brazil a
que se procedeu no dia 1° de Agosto de 1872 (apparently the only
copy in this country), publications from later censuses and the
central government's compilation of vital statistics. For the
states there is generally the Sinópse Estatística do [s] Município [s] [do] Estado and the state's own statistical annual or equi-
valent. Yale's resources included the censuses since 1890, other
national statistical publications and a limited number of annuals,
bulletin, and other compilations issued by the states.

Other government publications are well represented at Library of Congress (35, 106). New York Public (7) also has a
strong collection, expecially for the twentieth century. Harvard's
holdings of general documents are less substantial than those of
law, but nevertheless occupy ten sections of shelving in the School
of Public Administration. Pan American Union has good coverage
of official publications, which constitute one of the chief forms of
new accessions. Another strong collection is maintained by
California (Berkeley), which holds, for example, the Relatório of
the Ministério de Fazenda (1835-1906) and of the Ministério das
Relações Exteriores (1855-1949, with gaps), while the Oliveira
Lima set of the latter runs from the first issued to about 1940.

Wisconsin's collection is only fair; some years ago it de-
posited a number of Brazilian documents in the Midwest Inter-
Library Center. The agencies best represented are Conselho
Nacional de Estatística, Conselho Nacional de Geografia, Depart-
amento Nacional de Produção Mineral, and three Ministérios--
Agricultura, Educação e Saúde Pública and Relações Exteriores.

Florida is currently receiving 383 serial titles of the federal
government and the state of Guanabara (former federal district),
and Pennsylvania holds some two hundred titles. Iowa has concentrated on documents which provide statistical information, a type
in which California (Los Angeles) is also interested, in addition to

those of an administrative, legal, and economic nature. Oklahoma reports a number of publications, several of them from the Departamento Nacional de Produção Mineral, and Southern California collected official publications heavily from 1945 to 1953.

NEWSPAPERS, JOURNALISM, AND GENERAL PERIODICALS

Only two libraries--California (Los Angeles) and Florida--mention their current newspaper subscriptions. Both receive O Estado de São Paulo and Correio da Manhã; the former subscribes to two additional titles from Rio de Janeiro (Diário de Notícias and O Jornal), while Florida has received Correio do Povo from Porto Alegre since 1954.

Although there is a union list of holdings of Latin American newspapers (83), the fact that it is now ten years old probably means that it is no longer either complete or accurate. However, it is unlikely that the picture of scattered holdings of individual issues of the newspapers of smaller cities has changed. Even these tend to be concentrated in such libraries as American Antiquarian, Illinois, Library of Congress, New York Public, Pan American Union, and Wisconsin. For Rio de Janeiro at least seven significant runs existed when the union list appeared: Correio da Manhã since 1943 at Illinois and since 1949 at Texas; O Jornal since 1947 at New York Public; Jornal do Commércio since 1944 at Pan American Union, since 1949 at Library of Congress and Wisconsin, and since 1950 at Illinois.

More up-to-date information (39) for southern libraries shows, however, few significant runs aside from those already mentioned, except for Jornal do Brasil from 1923 to 1945 (with gaps) at North Carolina, Rio News from 1883 to 1897 (with gaps) at Florida, and Jornal do Commércio since 1946 at Louisiana.

Titles on microfilm (110) do not add significantly to these resources; aside from some single issues and short runs in the nineteenth century, most tend to duplicate the above. Moreover, the bulk of work has been done for newspapers in Rio de Janeiro and São Paulo; the only others reported are A Folha do Norte (Belém) and Correio do Povo (Porto Alegre); apparently such important cities as Bahia, Belo Horizonte, Curitiba, Fortaleza, and Recife are not represented.

No information is available on Brazilian journalism, except for Library of Congress, which has thirty-three titles. They include several items on newspapers outside of Rio de Janeiro and on the German language press.

Information on periodical holdings generally relates to the ninety-eight titles on the Zimmerman list. As pointed out in the introductory note to Appendix 2 (p. 105), no attempt was made to enlarge the number of titles, even though some libraries have reported additional titles which they are receiving.

The sixty-three libraries that reported on serials have an indicated total of 1,359 files for the ninety-eight titles (this figure counts each reported holding as one, taking no account of its completeness). One or more libraries receive each title, but the range is from a single to forty-six subscriptions, with an average of fourteen per title.

No single library receives all the periodicals listed, but each of seven institutions holds more than half. They are, in descending order, Pan American Union 85; Library of Congress 83; Texas 72; California (Berkeley) 62; Florida 60; New York Public 57; and Harvard 50. This would seem to demonstrate that widest coverage, in terms of number of titles, is found in the largest libraries and in those which have stressed development of Latin American holdings.

Comments on periodicals in specific fields appear at the end of the respective sections, but there remain fifteen titles that are general in nature or cover several subjects. Observations on holdings and availability of these titles follow. They are not widely held, with a few exceptions like Anhembi (P4)* (1950-1962), which has now ceased publication. Of the seventeen libraries reporting subscriptions four--Florida, Joint University Libraries, Pan American Union, and Wisconsin--have all issues, while Illinois and Library of Congress lack one and two numbers respectively. A complete file of O Cruzeiro (P30) (1928-   ) is apparently unavailable in this country, although the collection at Library of Congress begins in 1939 and Florida, Illinois, Michigan, Missouri, Pan American Union, and Texas subscribe on a current basis; the Illinois set of the international edition (P31) (1957-   ) commences with volume 3. A similar situation obtains for Seleções do Reader's Digest (P91) (1942-   ), for which Library of Congress holds the first twenty-four volumes and only Florida State, Oregon, and New Mexico receive current issues. Collections at Harvard and Utah include all volumes of Brazilian American Survey (P23) (1953-   ), while those at California (Berkeley), Duke, Florida, Kansas, Library of Congress, New York Public, Oregon, Pan American Union, Stanford, and Yale lack the early years. California (Berkeley), Pan American Union, and Wisconsin have

---

* Numbers in parentheses preceded by P refer to the periodical's number in Appendix 2.

assembled complete files of the Revista do Instituto Brasil-
Estados Unidos (P76)(1943-). At New York Public and Pan American Union there are full sets of Brasil Moderno (P21) (1951-),
and at the same institutions and Harvard, of Arquivos Brasileiros
de Psicotécnica (P6) (1949-); at California (Berkeley), Florida,
and Pan American Union, of Correio de IBECC (P29) (1958-);
at Pan American Union, of Mundo Melhor (P49) (1958-); and at
California (Los Angeles), of Manchete (P45) (1952-). California (Berkeley) and Texas have acquired the 1961/62 issue of
Anuário da Imprensa, Rádio, e Televisão (P5) (1940-), and the
former subscribes on a current basis. No American library has
apparently assembled complete files of the remaining three periodicals; Pan American Union has the best collection of Revista
Esso (P87) (1945-) and Revista da Semana (P64) (1889-), although the latter set commences only in 1950; Library of Congress
and Stanford have best holdings of Visão (P97) (1952-), but
several early years are lacking in both cases.

BIBLIOGRAPHY AND LIBRARY SCIENCE

As one might expect, there is widespread interest in acquiring bibliographical tools. Strong collections have been formed at
Library of Congress (over seventy-five titles, embracing all important monographic and serial publications, classified as Brazilian national bibliography), Oliveira Lima Library at Catholic University, Pan American Union, Texas (215 volumes, including all
major titles, with twenty-seven added in the past two years),
Cornell (134 volumes), and Florida (nearly 100 titles). While
present resources at Illinois are mostly from the last twenty
years, the Library now attempts to obtain all current publications.
Most of the standard tools are available at Newberry; the published bibliography covers holdings up to 1953 (67). A detailed,
if now dated, description of Duke's holdings has appeared (51).
Cleveland Public, Iowa, Joint University Libraries, Louisiana,
Michigan, Northwestern, Tulane, Virginia, and Yale report
smaller holdings.

As examples of individual titles Catholic, Cleveland Public,
Duke, Newberry, Stanford, and Yale hold José Carlos Rodrigues's
Bibliotheca Brasiliense, while Catholic, Cleveland Public, Duke,
Iowa, Kansas, Library of Congress, Newberry, Wisconsin, and
Yale have Augusto V. A. do Sacramento Blake's seven-volume
Diccionario Bibliographico Brazileiro. Complete sets of the Anais
of the Biblioteca Nacional in Rio de Janeiro are found at Cleveland
Public, Iowa, Newberry, Texas, Yale (and undoubtedly in other
institutions as well); Oliveira Lima's set is almost complete,

while Florida, Miami, and Syracuse report long, but incomplete, files.

In the area of book industries and trade, Library of Congress has acquired a dozen titles on printing, publishing and bookselling, and copyright. For the history of books and printing Indiana's Mendel Collection contains over twenty Rio de Janeiro imprints for 1808, the year in which the first printing press was established in Brazil. The publications of the Sociedade dos Cem Bibliófilos do Brasil provide splendid examples of deluxe modern printing; Library of Congress (17) lacks only one of the seventeen volumes that appeared between 1944 and 1963. Issued in limited editions of 119 (later 120) copies--one of which is reserved for the Library--these handsome volumes consist of reprints of Brazilian classics with illustrations by such Brazilian artists as Portinari, Clovis Graciano, and Iberê Camargo.

In contrast, only a few institutions mentioned library science separately as a field of strength. One of the best collections is located at Columbia's School of Library Service Library-- seventy-five titles, most of them listed in its published catalog (20). The School attempts to acquire all current publications relating to library science and documentation (including those of the Brazilian Institute of Bibliography and Documentation). Pan American Union (74, 78) probably has the best current receipts of any American library, at least of non-book items, due to its many contacts with librarians in Latin America and its Library Development Program. About seventy-five titles available at Library of Congress comprise publications of the National Library, directories, monographic works on library history, development, and the like, together with catalogs of numerous libraries (chiefly those in Rio de Janeiro). Since 1956 the Library Science Library at Illinois has added items relating to the binational center libraries in Brazil, the second and third Brazilian Bibliography and Documentation Congresses (1959 and 1961), and miscellaneous ephemeral material about specific library schools and libraries.

Of four important serials in the field, two--the Boletim Bibliográfico (P8) (1951-) of the Biblioteca Nacional and the same title of the São Paulo Biblioteca Municipal (P9) (1943-) are quite widely held. Thirty libraries report the former and thirty-nine the latter, with complete sets of both available at California (Berkeley), Harvard, Library of Congress, Miami, New York Public, Pan American Union, Stanford, Texas, Wisconsin, and Yale. The Boletim Informativo (P19) (1955-) of the Brazilian Institute of Bibliography and Documentation (IBBD) can be found at fewer institutions, and the fourteen reporting libraries are con-

centrated in California, District of Columbia, Florida, Kentucky,
New York, and Texas. No library has indicated a complete set
of the <u>Boletim da Biblioteca da Câmara dos Deputados</u> (P11)
1952-   ).

◆3 Humanities

PHILOSOPHY AND RELIGION

It appears that American research libraries have, to date, paid but slight attention to Brazilian philosophy, perhaps because as one curator put it, "Brazilians are not theoretically inclined." Although the larger collections devoted to Brazilian studies probably include titles in this field, there is little specific mention of holdings. Library of Congress has about fifty titles, two-thirds of them the works of individual philosophers. New York University possesses about thirty titles; Texas recently added four volumes published in 1960; Yale has six books published between 1943 and 1957. For current material Illinois has received books issued since beginning its Farmington Plan coverage of Brazil in 1961, and Wisconsin added this subject to its blanket order in 1963. Eleven libraries indicate holdings of the Revista Brasileira de Filosofia (P57) (1951-), a figure which seems to bear out this lack of interest; only four sets (California at Berkeley, Library of Congress, New York Public, and Pan American Union) appear to be complete.

Although religion fares somewhat better, it has not evoked widespread interest either, and strong holdings seem to be limited to the colonial period. At Duke (51) there is material about the three great missionaries who worked in Brazil--José de Anchieta, Manuel da Nobrega, and Antonio de Vieira; items at Newberry (67) include a dozen by and about Anchieta and about the same number on Vieira. Included in the collection of about a thousand Portuguese pamphlets acquired in 1954 is a sermon which Vieira preached in 1640 in Bahia (59). The Hull Collection at Cornell(87) contains material about the Jesuit missions and their influence, and the Oliveira Lima Library at Catholic University (14) is strong in Brazilian church history and especially rich in Jesuit letters and relations. It contains, for example, the important source for Jesuit activities in Brazil, Les Lettres édifiantes et curieuses écrites des missions étrangères par quelques missionaires de la Compagnie de Jesús (26v.;1736) and the scarce complete set of Vieira's Sermões (16v.;1679-1754). The former can also be found at Stanford. Texas also has material on the Catholic Church in America; along with Newberry and Yale it reports Serafim Leite's history of the Jesuits in Brazil (10v.;1938). New York Public (29) has a small number of volumes on religious fanaticism in Brazil, including studies on Antonio Conselheiro and Padre Cicero. Also available are works on the African religions brought to Brazil.

Holdings on religion at Library of Congress amount to about one hundred titles, probably half of them dealing with the Catholic Church. Among these are works on specific archdioceses, monasteries and churches as well as general histories. Almost as many works concern missionary activities, especially those of protestant groups (e.g., Baptists and Methodists) in the Amazon Valley in the twentieth century; many are in the nature of personal reminiscences. In contrast, there are no books specifically about Judaism in Brazil.

Of the four journals in this field listed by Zimmerman two are published by Catholic universities: Verbum (P95) (1944-) by the Catholic University of Rio de Janeiro and Veritas (P96) (1955-) by the Catholic University of Rio Grande do Sul. A complete set of the former is available at California (Berkeley) and Notre Dame's starts with volume 2; of the latter California (Berkeley) and Harvard report all volumes. Indicated holdings of the two remaining titles--Vozes (P98) and A Ordem (P52) are even more limited. The former began publication in 1907, and apparently the best file is available at Library of Congress. The latter commenced in 1921, but early years are not found in an American library. Volumes at Catholic University, Library of Congress, and Pan American Union give the Washington area the most nearly complete collection.

FINE ARTS

The Library of Congress has strong holdings in the fine arts, including books, serials, and special materials. In the general collection (Class N) there are over one hundred titles, the bulk of them on architecture and painting. Significant groups in the former cover architecture in Brazil since 1940 and religious architecture (15 titles), especially the churches of Minas Gerais and Bahia.

There are a dozen works about city planning (chiefly on Rio de
Janeiro). Material on painting includes historical studies, catalogs of exhibitions and works on such contemporary figures as
Portinari and Lula Cardoso Ayres. A small group deals with
sculpture with some additional titles on individual figures (e.g.,
"Aleijadinho"). Although the Library of Congress Classification
makes ample provision for decoration and ornament (Class NK),
practically no books dealing with Brazil have entered the collection. There are about twenty-five titles on the stage in Brazil,
including some devoted to the theatre in Bahia and Rio de Janeiro
and to Brazilian actors and actresses.

The unusual feature of these resources consists of extensive
illustrative material located in the Prints and Photographs Division (112-b, 112-d, 118). In the Archives of Hispanic Culture there
are two file drawers of photographs devoted to church and civil
architecture in Brazilian cities. Not limited to general views,
the pictures often show architectural detail. The states of Bahia,
Pernambuco, Minas Gerais, Sao Paulo, and Guanabara are best
covered; only occasional items come from the others. Over fifty
photographs of churches and historical buildings of Ouro Preto and
twenty-five of Sao Paulo in 1860, the latter embracing many buildings since razed, possess more than routine value. The Archive
also contains 1 1/2 file drawers of reproductions of works of
about fifty artists; Portinari alone is represented by nearly one
hundred. There is a slide collection of selected paintings and
buildings of architectural interest.

A collection of drawings on civil architecture in colonial
Minas Gerais and Sao Paulo by José W. Rodrigues consists of
forty plates, each with several drawings of structural details and
ornaments. In 1958 Anita Moore, wife of Rear Admiral F. R.
Moore, USN, augmented these holdings when she presented to the
Library her collection of 220 color photographs of Brazilian art
objects and architecture, together with her descriptions and notes
on the art of Brazil. The Robert C. Smith Collection, Brazilian
Architecture Documents, includes diazo prints and enlargements
from microcopies of archival plans, drawings, and tracings relating to historic monuments, churches, and other buildings in
Brazil and to their preservation and restoration, copies from
originals in the archives of the Serviço do Patrimônio Histórico e
Artístico Nacional.

Other special collections in this Division offer pictorial material of a topical nature. As might be expected, coffee figures
prominently, but there are also groups of photographs on highways
(1932-1940), hydroelectric plants (ca. 1940), the steel mill at

Volta Redonda, the Amazon health program (1942), the Sao Paulo
YMCA (1925), and regional costumes (1952). Other groups depict
life in various regions--e.g., Minas Gerais (one collection from
1891 and another from a half century later), Bahia (1951), reproductions of the drawings of José Lutzenberger of the gaúchos of
Rio Grande do Sul, and various collections devoted to Rio de Janeiro. Of a more general nature one finds in the Carpenter collection about 125 mounted photographs dating from the 1920's of
cities (Rio de Janeiro, Sao Paulo, Bahia, and Recife) and agriculture and in the Miscellaneous File about ninety mounted photographs, some from the Office of the Co-ordinator of Inter-American Affairs; they depict chiefly Rio de Janeiro and Sao Paulo in the
1940's. Two additional files (Fine Prints and Portraits) also contain Brazilian items, but since both are organized by name rather
than by country it is not possible to report on the specific nature
and extent of holdings.

Also found in Washington, in the Oliveira Lima Library (95),
is a collection of ten watercolor drawings by Francisco Requena,
made during his journey as leader of the Spanish commission to
the Amazon (1778-1790) under the Spanish-Portuguese Treaty of
1777. Although there is evidence to support the belief that Requena's watercolors are part of a larger series (consisting of at
least seventeen items), the surviving pictures portray two scenes
of preparation for the journey, showing the use of rafts and the
making of a canoe; two views of Maynas missions visited by the
Spanish commission en route down the Amazon; and six episodes
from the expedition up the Japurá and its tributaries. The Oliveira Lima collection also reports complete sets of the publications of the Serviço do Patrimônio Histórico e Artístico Nacional
and the Anais of the Museu Imperial.

The most valuable single item in Cornell's Hull Collection
(87) is a set of unique watercolors made in Rio de Janeiro in the
1820's. Done by Robert Bate, a successful English businessman
who found time to sketch in watercolors during his stay in Rio de
Janeiro from 1807 to 1821 and during five more trips to Brazil,
they portray the cultural and architectural history of the city as
capital of the Brazilian Empire.

The Hispanic Society (94) has paintings and drawings by
Franz Frühbeck. Other resources in New York City are excellent,
with publications available at the New York Public Library (some
37 entries under "Art, Brazilian" in the Art Division catalog); an
unusually fine collection at New York University's Institute of
Fine Arts; and a dozen titles on the history of Brazilian painting
and sculpture at Columbia's Fine Arts Library. The Metropolitan

Museum's holdings (64, 65) embrace general works on Brazilian
art, painting, and a small group on architecture.

Illinois buys actively in this field, and Michigan has strengthened its holdings on Brazilian painting, sculpture, and architecture in the past twenty years and now has twenty titles on architecture alone. More limited amounts of material are available at
Iowa, Joint University Libraries, Louisiana, Minnesota, Newberry, Northwestern, and Oklahoma. In contrast, Wisconsin's
holdings are weak, consisting mainly of general works. There
are practically no titles about individual artists and architects,
little on the various regions (except for Rio de Janeiro and Sao
Paulo) and no catalogs of exhibits, of permanent or special collections or of annual and biennial salons.

Resources of Columbia's Avery Library (19) consist of approximately sixty titles, current and historical, on Brazilian
architecture, housing and city and regional planning. It contains
complete sets of the Publicações and Revista of the Patrimônio
Histórico e Artístico Nacional. The Library of Congress, Texas,
and Yale also have unbroken files of the Revista (P83) (1937-);
shorter runs are available in numerous other collections. All
volumes of the two important art journals Habitat (P48) (1950-)
and Módulo (P40) (1955-) are present at California (Berkeley);
of the former at Harvard (except volume 1), Pan American Union
and Pennsylvania and of the latter at Georgia Institute of Technology. Nearly complete collections of Habitat can be consulted at
Louisiana and Minnesota; of Módulo at Connecticut, Illinois, Library of Congress, New York Public, Stanford, and Washington
(St. Louis).

MUSIC

The Music Division of the Library of Congress has probably
assembled the outstanding collection of Brazilian music in this
country. Resources covering general works, biography and criticism, lyric theatre, music education, instruction and theory, the
national anthem, folk and primitive music (including Amerindian
and Afro-Brazilian) and popular music are represented in Chase's
Guide to the Music of Latin America (15); the Library's call numbers are given (except for entries in the second part, most of
which are probably also present in the collections).

For history and criticism of Brazilian music there are forty-
two volumes in the classified holdings (ML232) including some
works on music in the various regions of Brazil and on the influ-

ence of Portuguese music on Brazilian.   There are such bibliographical items as Azevedo's <u>Bibliografia Musical Brasileira</u> and
<u>150 Anos de Música no Brasil</u>.

Sheet music and scores include twenty-two collections of
both national and regional works (e.g., Northeast, Bahia, and
gaúcho). For modern Brazilian composers there are thirty-three
items by Camargo Guarnieri, including the holograph of his
<u>Brasiliana;</u> twenty-four by Francisco Mignon; two by Luiz Cosme,
as well as four of his books. Of course best represented is
Heitor Villa-Lobos, for whom there are three hundred musical
items (not, however, including any holographs) and six biographical and critical studies. Resources also include popular songs
from Brazil, which have come as copyright deposits. Although
received since 1939, probably 80 per cent have arrived after 1955.
They include sambas, fados, boleros, tangos , and bossa novas
with numerous examples by such composers as João Maria de
Abreu, Ary Baroso, and Tito Madio. Among the Brazilian periodicals found in the collections are <u>Música Viva</u>, <u>Resenha Musical</u>,
<u>Revista da Associação Brasileira de Música</u>, <u>Revista Brasileira
de Música</u>, <u>Brasil Musical</u>, <u>Música Sacra</u> and <u>Música</u>, <u>Revista da
Fundação Orquesta Filarmônica de São Paulo</u>.

At the Pan American Union there is a collection of sheet
music and scores now amounting to 2,500 pieces, including some
750 items presented by the Brazilian government. A small part
of these, including piano solos, part songs, chamber music, and
works for violin and piano, band and orchestra, was   listed some
years ago (50). The Oliveria Lima Library at Catholic University also reports a fine collection of Brazilian music.

At Columbia there is a good working collection, including
books, serials, and records representative of contemporary
music (some of them unobtainable through commercial channels).
The Library emphasizes the history of Brazilian music and description and analysis of folk music and other music types.

A number of works on folk music , including songs of African origin and from the interior of various states, is available at
New York Public (29), but Wisconsin's holdings in this area comprise only a few basic works, which would be insufficient to support research.

The William Sewall Marsh Collection of Spanish and Latin
American Music at Brown contains some material on Brazil.
There are now more than three hundred pieces of sheet music by
Brazilian composers at Indiana, and its Institute of Latin Ameri-

can Music is buying heavily in the field. In 1953 Newberry's holdings (67) included fifteen monographs and the Revista Brasileira de
Música.

Only four libraries--Illinois, Library of Congress, Pan
American Union, and Utah--possess Música Sacra (P50) (1940-),
of which the Library of Congress alone has a complete set.

LANGUAGE AND LITERATURE

The description which follows shows that Brazilian literature
probably constitutes the subject best represented in American libraries. The teaching of literature courses on university campus-
es has unquestionably stimulated the development of resources in
this field.

However, from available information it would appear that
few libraries have acquired special materials on the Portuguese
language in Brazil. Texas does have excellent linguistics holdings
(259 volumes), and faculty interest at Illinois has aided in obtaining
two hundred volumes. There are one hundred titles on peninsular
and Brazilian Portuguese at Joint University Libraries and the
same number at Library of Congress devoted to the language in
Brazil. In the latter collection the following topics are well
represented: the divergence of Brazilian Portuguese from that of
Portugal, influences on the Brazilian language (e.g., African and
Indian), and regionalisms (especially those of the northeast and
south); there are also dictionaries of Brazilianisms and texts for
learning the language. California (Los Angeles) and Oliveira Lima
Library at Catholic University have good collections of dictionaries. On the other hand, at Michigan and Wisconsin holdings are
only average, although at Wisconsin works treating Brazilian
dialects have received some emphasis.

Although it is difficult to compare collections from either a
qualitative or a quantitative approach, use of two devices brought
together some useful information. The first tabulates the holdings
reported by twenty-eight libraries (Table II). Because methods of
counting vary widely and because some libraries report in terms
of volumes and some in terms of titles, these figures are of more
value in indicating relative size than in permitting one to determine
a rank order. The second utilized Moser's list of histories of
Brazilian literature* as a sample for checking the availability of

---

* Gerald M. Moser, "Histories of Brazilian Literature; A Critical Survey,"
  Inter-American Review of Bibliography, X (1960), 117-146.

such works in this country. After eliminating serial items, dis-
sertations, and works cited in several editions, ninety-one monographic works remained (of 111 listed). Checking the National
Union Catalog reveals that, while American libraries lack only
three items (Table III), forty-five titles (just under half of the
total) are held by fewer than six libraries. (It is of course quite
possible that the National Union Catalog fails to indicate all copies
of these works that are actually in this country.) Of these less
generally available items twenty-eight institutions have acquired
a total of 146 copies (Table IV). It is interesting to note that if
one starts with the twenty-six titles available at Library of Congress and adds the non-duplicating works of the other libraries
in the order in which they appear in Table IV, it will require seven
additional institutions to secure complete coverage of all forty-
five histories: Wisconsin adds seven, Texas five, California
(Berkeley) and Catholic two each, New York Public, Yale, and
Chicago one each. Although the limited size of the sample does
not warrant generalization, it would seem to indicate that extensive duplication of resources has not taken place, even of such
standard items as histories of literature.

Four types of literature collections exist: those of a general
or comprehensive nature and those emphasizing the colonial
period, the nineteenth and twentieth centuries, and the contemporary period.

Of the general collections the one formed at Library of
Congress surpasses all others in extent of holdings. For literary
history and criticism there are approximately four hundred titles.
Works of standard authors--e.g., Ronald de Carvalho, Afrânio
Coutinho, Isaac Goldberg, Álvaro Lins, Samuel Putnam, Sílvio
Romero, to name but a few--are present; of special genres poetry
is well covered (thirty-eight titles by Manuel Bandeira and others).
Among the individual topics on which monographs appear are
women as authors, slavery and crime in Brazilian literature, and
the influence of the Indian and the Negro. It might be noted that
there are numerous publications in the collection known as "The
Portuguese Pamphlets" reflecting the Camões tercentenary cele-
brations in Brazil (85, 105-d).

About sixty titles, chiefly histories and anthologies, deal
with regional literature, and coverage is most extensive for the
Northeast, Minas Gerais, Sao Paulo, and Rio Grande do Sul.

The bulk of the collection (approximately 3, 300 titles) consists of works of individual authors. The classification divides
them into three series: writers prior to 1800, those of the nine-

TABLE II

HOLDINGS OF BRAZILIAN LITERATURE IN 28 LIBRARIES

Library	Volumes or Titles*
Brown	200[a]
Catholic	2,200*
Columbia	1,200
Cornell	550
Duke	1,375
Emory	110
Florida	530*
Harvard	2,000[b]
Illinois	2,000
Indiana	200*
Iowa	100
Joint University	900*
Kansas	150
Library of Congress	3,700*
Louisiana	200*
Michigan	500*
Minnesota	340*
New Mexico	2,500[c]
New York Public	1,830*
Northwestern	550
Ohio State	200
Oklahoma	200[c]
Princeton	600
Texas	2,200
Tulane	110
Virginia	100
Wisconsin	1,240[d]
Yale	660*

[a] Excludes poetry in Harris Collection
[b] Includes bibliography, dictionaries, criticism, and works of individual authors
[c] Includes philology
[d] Excludes works not yet in Library of Congress classification

NOTE: Most figures are approximate

SOURCES: Data supplied by libraries

teenth century and the first half of the twentieth, and those from the second half of the twentieth century to date (defined as authors beginning to publish around 1950, flourishing after 1960). In quantity the first contains less than fifty titles, the second about 3,100, and the third approximately 150.

Comments on holdings of selected major authors follow. Of those for the period prior to 1800, resources are most extensive for Tomás Antônio Gonzaga--twenty works by and about him; all, however, are modern editions. For José de Alencar there are forty-nine editions and seven critical studies; the earliest of the nine editions of Iracema is 1865, but a first edition of O gaúcho is present. For Castro Alves twenty-five critical studies by such authors as Pedro Calmon, Edison Carneiro, Afrânio Peixoto, and Jamil Almansur Haddad outnumber the twenty-one editions of his works. For Gonçalves Dias there are seventeen editions (of which two date from the nineteenth century) and seven critical studies. Monteiro Lobato figures more prominently in the Library's collection of Brazilian juvenile literature than any other author, but a dozen titles and three critical studies are classified with literature. The largest collection comprises works by and about Machado de Assis. Of the seventy-nine editions present, only three were published during his lifetime--the third of Quincas Borba, the Paris edition of Yayá Garcia and an inscribed copy of his comedy, Tu só, tu, puro amor (85), and there are English and French translations of some of his best known works. About fifty biographical and critical studies include general studies, those about special aspects of his life and work, and those on individual writings. Other authors represented in the Library's collections by a substantial number of editions are Guilherme de Almeida, Aluízio Azevedo, Olavo Bilac, Coelho Netto, Alfredo d'Escragnolle Taunay, Menotti del Picchia, Alberto de Oliveira, and Afrânio Peixoto. In 1941 the Library (105-f) received from Afonso d'Escragnolle Taunay 271 volumes and 261 pamphlets of his works and other publications on Brazilian literature and history. For authors writing since 1950 there are generally only one or two titles each; the following comprise some representative names: Ana Maria Amarel, Ricardo Brandão, Osório Alves de Casto, Colbert Rangel Coelho, Oscar Negrão de Lima, Rodrigues Marques, Victor Pedroso, Zálkind Piatigórsky, Paulo Emílio Pinto, José Newton Alves de Sousa.

At least three Brazilians are represented in the collection of recordings of Hispanic writers reading their works: Manuel Bandeira, Ascensio Ferreira, and Jorge de Lima (112-c).

TABLE III

DUPLICATION OF HOLDINGS OF 91 HISTORIES
OF BRAZILIAN LITERATURE

Held By	Number of Titles	Per Cent
10 or more libraries	20	21.9
9 libraries	6	6.6
8 libraries	4	4.4
7 libraries	9	9.9
6 libraries	4	4.4
5 libraries	6	6.6
4 libraries	17	18.7
3 libraries	8	8.8
2 libraries	10	11.0
1 library	4	4.4
No library	3	3.3
TOTAL	91	100.0

SOURCE: Data obtained by checking National Union Catalog and
University of Wisconsin Library Catalog

Among the larger collections, Harvard's contains five
hundred volumes of bibliographies, histories of literature, and the
like, and 1,500 of works of individual authors. Annual donations
from the Brazilian Embassy which contain literary productions
and periodicals have augmented holdings for the contemporary
period at the New York Public (9). The collection now contains
over 1,800 titles, of which 120 are collections and anthologies,
while about 1,700 are works of individual authors, divided as follows: fiction 900, poetry 420, drama 270, and essays 120.

Holdings of the Oliveira Lima Library at Catholic University extend over all periods and genres of Brazilian literature, but are especially strong for the period from 1822 to about 1930. They include the standard critical titles and complete works of Machado de Assis, Aluízio Azevedo, Coelho Netto, Júlia Lopes de Almeida, Sílvio Romero, José Veríssimo, Ruy Barbosa, Joaquim Nabuco, Euclides da Cuna, João Ribeiro, and others. Also in Washington the Pan American Union collection is strong in literature and covers all periods from the colonial to the contemporary.

Resources at Texas are outstanding with 2,200 volumes. They increase by several hundred books annually, and new accessions cover all periods, including new editions and criticism of such major figures as Machado de Assis, José de Alencar, José Lins do Rego, and others.

Statistics for Brazilian literature at Wisconsin are incomplete, because the Library has only partially reclassified from Cutter to Library of Congress. In the latter group (about 1,240 volumes excluding serials) the authors best represented include José de Alencar, Gilberto Amado, Mário de Andade, Manuel Bandeira, Castro Alves, Afonso Lima Barreto, Jorge de Lima, Ruy Ribeiro Couto, Machado de Assis and Menotti del Picchia. Additional holdings remain in about eight hundred volumes of Portuguese language material still classified in Cutter. Of the 111 literary histories on the Moser list the Library holds 90 or 81 per cent; some of those not present appeared in the nineteenth century.

Yale's collection of literary histories includes such nineteenth century titles as Wolf's Brésil Littéraire and Perié's Litteratura Brasileira nos Tempos Coloniaes. Of the earlier writers best represented are Alencar (17 titles), Machado de Assis and Alfredo d'Escragnolle Taunay. Approximately half of the collection, however, consists of twentieth century authors with Jorge Amado, Gustavo Barroso, Coelho Netto, Graça Aranha, Lima Barreto, and Jose Lins do Rêgo well covered.

The collection at Florida (530 titles) embraces the major histories of literature, some critical studies, representative colonial writers, poets, and other figures of the nineteenth and twentieth centuries (including complete works of the most important), but it emphasizes the Brazilian novel, with complete or nearly complete works of Machado de Assis, José Lins do Rêgo, Jorge Amado, Graciliano Ramos, Érico Veríssimo, José de Alencar, Aluízio Azevedo, etc. St. Louis University has also stressed this genre, with attention paid especially to four novelists:

TABLE IV

HOLDINGS OF 45 HISTORIES OF BRAZILIAN LITERATURE
IN SELECTED LIBRARIES

Library	Number of Titles Held
Library of Congress	26
Wisconsin	26
Texas	13
California (Berkeley)	12
Harvard	9
Illinois	8
New York Public	8
Catholic University	7
Pan American Union	6
Michigan	4
Duke	3
Newberry	3
Yale	3
Others*	18
TOTAL	146**

*Two each: Cleveland Public, Chicago, Indiana; one each:
California (Los Angeles), Colorado, Cornell, Kansas,
Louisiana State, North Carolina, Northwestern, Pennsyl-
vania, Princeton, University of the City of New York,
Union Theological and Virginia
**Total number of copies

SOURCE: Same as Table III

Machado de Assis, José de Alencar, Jorge Amado, and José Lins do Rêgo.

Extensive holdings at California (Berkeley) consist, in part, of excellent representation of the works of the following authors: José de Alencar, Mário de Andrade, Aluízio Azevedo, Euclides da Cunha, Afonso and Alfredo d'Escragnolle Taunay, Gonçalves Dias, José Pereira da Graça Aranha, Álvaro Lins, Machado de Assis, Cecília Meireles, Joaquim Nabuco, Sílvio Romero, Affonso Schmidt, and José Veríssimo. The acquisition program calls for complete coverage of important living authors (e. g., Jorge Amado, Gilberto Freyre, Alceu-Amoroso Lima, José Lins do Rêgo, Graciliano Ramos, and Érico Veríssimo). The collection is strong in the literature both of the Northeast and of the southern part of the country.

The collection at Syracuse is a general one. The following authors are best represented: José de Alencar, Jorge Amado, Aluízio Azevedo, Ruy Barbosa, Castro Alves, Gonçalves Dias, José Lins do Rêgo, Machado de Assis, Lúcia Miguel Pereira, Afrânio Peixoto and Érico Veríssimo.

Brown reports about two hundred volumes of Brazilian literature but points out that its Harris Collection of American Poetry and Plays contains about 2,300 volumes of Latin American poetry, some of which would be Brazilian. At Oklahoma holdings of history and criticism amount to about forty volumes, fiction to one hundred, and poetry to ninety.

Two libraries have concentrated on the colonial period. The Hispanic Society does not attempt to develop its resources for later periods. In 1953 Newberry's holdings (67) numbered some fifty-five titles, embracing a number of works of history and criticism and works of major writers; this reflects the fact that, although William B. Greenlee was interested in literature, he collected much more heavily in the field of history and emphasized Brazil as a colony of Portugal.

Turning now to those collections which stress the nineteenth and twentieth centuries, one finds large holdings (approximately 1,200 titles) at Columbia. The Library holds the more important bibliographical compilations, historical and critical studies, as well as collected works of major figures. Resources are stronger for the nineteenth and early twentieth centuries than for the contemporary period. The same holds true for New York University. California (Los Angeles) reports the principal writings and important secondary works for this period. Emory, Indiana, and North Carolina also emphasize this period, while Northwestern and Pennsylvania have stressed the period after independence. The former has 550 volumes, and the latter's holdings include 125 titles of history, criticism, and bibliography.

A number of libraries have specialized in contemporary literature. Although Michigan has not stressed Portuguese studies, the Library has built up collections of Brazilian prose and poetry, especially works published around 1940. Of Minnesota's 340 titles about 85 per cent represent material for the period since 1940; there are, for example, twenty-two titles by or about Érico Veríssimo, twelve by or about José Lins do Rêgo, fifteen by or about Paulo Setubal and fifteen by or about Jorge Amado. The total includes about sixty works of history and criticism and thirty-five anthologies. Large holdings (2,000 volumes) at Illinois are strong in this period; Joint University Libraries have tried to acquire the works of major writers of the twentieth century. Although the six hundred volumes by Brazilian authors in the circulating Portuguese language collection at Cleveland Public cover a variety of subjects, they contain the best modern Brazilian writers (e.g., Euclides da Cunha, José Lins do Rêgo, Érico Veríssimo) as well as such standard figures as Machado de Assis. About one hundred books at Tulane and at Iowa are mostly post-1940 imprints; the former is expanding its holdings, while Kansas has given attention in the past five years to acquiring works of well known contemporary authors.

Considering the strength of monographic holdings, it is somewhat surprising to find relatively few sets of journals. Revista do Livro (P80) (1956-) is complete at California (Berkeley), Harvard, Illinois, Library of Congress, Michigan, and Northwestern; Revista Brasiliense (P61) 1955-) at California (Berkeley), California (Los Angeles), Harvard, and Pan American Union; Revista da Academia Paulista de Letras (P62) (1937?-) at California (Berkeley), Pan American Union, and Stanford. Pan American Union has the only full set of Clã (P26) (1948-) and the most nearly complete of Jornal de Letras (P43) (1949-), although Illinois and Texas also have long runs of the latter. Of four files of Diálogo: Revista de Cultura (P32) (1955-) those at California (Berkeley) and Pan American Union are complete.

Social Sciences

ANTHROPOLOGY, FOLKLORE, AND SOCIOLOGY

In anthropology a great deal of the emphasis falls on materials about the Indians. Significant resources are available in
the Ayer Collection at Newberry(67, 68), and by 1963 it was estimated that the Library contained at least two hundred titles dealing in whole or in part with the Indians of Brazil. As examples
of the more unusual items one might cite the following: Directorio
que se deve observar nas povoaçoens dos Indios do Pará e Maranhão em quanto Sua Magestade não mandar o contrario (1758),
Chabert's Historical Account ... of the Savage Inhabitants of
Brazil (1823), and Coelho de Senna, Os indios do Brasil (1908).

The Library of Congress has over three hundred titles on
this topic. There are works on various aspects of Indian life--
e.g., art, dances, folklore, religion--and on specific tribes--
e.g., Apalakiri, Bororo, Carib, Cadioéo, and Tupinamaba (35
titles). Resources of Indian languages are strong, dating back to
the acquisition of the Schuller collection in 1913 (105-a, 105-b).
It contains vocabularies and other linguistic material (some in
manuscript) on certain tribes. Present holdings on Tupi and
Guarani, for instance, number over one hundred grammars,
treatises, dictionaries, and textbooks.

The Hull Collection at Cornell also has material on the
languages and customs of the aborigines (50 volumes in Class F
alone); Pennsylvania rates its resources in this area as strong;
and there are fifty-seven titles in the John G. White Department
of the Cleveland Public. A smaller collection at Iowa, including
material in German and French in addition to Portuguese and
English, covers various tribes and areas as well as numerous
facets of Indian life.

Florida's holdings of over 150 titles in anthropology emphasize cultural anthropology, particularly Indians. The Branner Collection at Stanford contains material on anthropology and ethnology. There are one hundred volumes at Virginia, fifty at Indiana and thirty at Kansas. Illinois is making efforts to improve its holdings in this field, at present only average, and Tulane continues to make purchases. Other libraries with resources in this area are New York University, Northwestern, and Oklahoma.

The interest of American libraries in this field is clearly revealed by the fact that at least eleven (California at Berkeley and at Los Angeles, Florida, Harvard, Illinois, Indiana, New Mexico, New York Public, Pan American Union, Pennsylvania, and Wisconsin) hold the Revista de Antropologia (P69) (1953-) from the first volume to date. Three museum anthropological publications are also well distributed, a total of over eighty sets being located. For the Museu Nacional's Boletim (P16) (nova série; Antropologia, 1942-) California (Berkeley), Duke, Florida, Illinois, Kansas, Library of Congress, Michigan, Minnesota, New York State Library and Pan American Union have complete collections; for Boletim do Museu Paraense Emilio Goeldi (P17) (1957-), Florida, Kansas, Louisiana State, Michigan, New York Public, Pennsylvania, Stanford, and Wisconsin; and for Revista do Museu Paulista (P82) (1947-), California (Berkeley), Cornell, Duke, Florida, Library of Congress, Pan American Union, Pennsylvania, Texas, and Yale.

The John G. White Department of the Cleveland Public Library has built up a collection of fifty-eight titles on Brazilian folklore, including some reportedly not held by the Biblioteca Nacional in Rio de Janeiro. Books are in Portuguese and other languages. Resources at New York Public (29) are strong. They cover all regions of the country, although literature on the Northeast is probably most extensive. Topics represented include superstitions, myths and legends, proverbs, Carnaval and other festivals, dances, and a large group devoted to the Negro. Many of the studies are descriptive rather than analytical. Travel literature and fiction containing observations on manners and customs supplement basic holdings.

Purchase of the Boggs Collection of Latin American folklore strengthened holdings at California (Los Angeles), and Texas (102) recently acquired volumes on the folklore of the Northeast, Bahia, Rio de Janeiro, Sao Paulo, and Rio Grande do Sul and some forty titles on witchcraft and spiritualism (chiefly publications which appeared in the last ten years). Smaller collections are located at Cornell, Joint University Libraries, and Tulane.

Twenty-nine libraries report holdings of <u>Revista do Arquivo</u>
<u>Municipal</u> (P72) (1934-) with a complete set at California (Berk-
eley) and long runs at Duke, Louisiana, Michigan, Pennsylvania,
Princeton, and Wisconsin. In contrast of the two sets of <u>Boletim</u>
<u>da Commissão Catarinense de Folclore</u> (P12) (1949-) only that
at California (Berkeley) is complete; three libraries reported
<u>Folclore</u> (P39) (1949-), of which Library of Congress has the
best set.

In the field of sociology one of the aspects of Brazilian civilization of greatest interest undoubtedly is the formation of the
Brazilian nationality, which has resulted not only from immigration but also from racial blending. The special collections at
Catholic University, Cornell, and Stanford all contain material
in this area. Cornell has volumes on European immigration in the
nineteenth century (e.g., Germans in Rio Grande do Sul) and also
on modern sociological investigations describing the blending of
the three races. At Library of Congress there are fifty titles
classified as immigration (e.g., of such groups as Germans,
Italians, and Japanese) and another hundred as elements in the population. Development of resources about the Germans in southern
Brazil goes back as far as 1940, when the Library began to receive histories, periodicals, almanacs and pamphlets in German
from this area (105-e).

Library of Congress contains a great deal of additional material in this field, much of it scattered through the classified collection, however. Fifty works cover general social conditions in
the country, and another dozen conditions in specific areas. There
is also material on marriage and divorce, protection and care of
children, charity and public welfare (including several reports on
the Santa Casa da Misericórdia) and twenty-seven titles on slavery
(general histories and studies and works on abolition). Holdings
on criminology consist chiefly of reports from major cities and
less than a dozen histories and monographs; New York Public (45)
has long collected in this area and holds a number of documents
from around the turn of the century.

Florida reports over 340 titles in sociology (most of them
published since 1940), including nearly all works available in
English. It has collected a majority of the many community studies and is strong in demography; good holdings in description and
travel material provide support through the social history data
they contain. Judging from recent acquisitions, coverage of this
field is also very good at Texas. The Oliveira Lima Library at
Catholic University and the Branner Collection at Stanford also
contain material on social conditions, and the Wisconsin catalog

lists about sixty works under the subject heading "Brazil--Social conditions." The National Agricultural Library has books on rural sociology and rural life; Tulane reports that its holdings deal mainly with the Northeast. Smaller collections are found at Joint University Libraries, Minnesota, Northwestern, Oklahoma, and Virginia, but Illinois has made little effort to acquire in this field.

Three important journals deserve mention. There are twenty-nine collections of Sociologia (P93) (1939-), of which those at Duke, Library of Congress, and Pan American Union are complete. Full sets of Boletim do Instituto Joaquim Nabuco de Pesquisas Sociais (P14) (1952-) are available at California (Berkeley), Harvard, Library of Congress and Pan American Union and of Boletim do Centro Latino Americano de Pesquisas em Ciências Sociais, now América Latina, (P13) (1958-) at Florida, Minnesota, and Pan American Union, with several other sets nearly complete.

EDUCATION

There is little evidence of notable resources in the field of education, with the exception of a few institutions in New York and Washington. Teachers College, Columbia University (96), places relatively more emphasis on secondary education, official educational statistics and other government publications and relatively less on teaching of specific subjects and on child study; it does not attempt actively to acquire serials issued by university institutes, departments or faculties of education, nor documents issued by the Brazilian states. Coverage of national educational statistics and official reports is good and of general publications fair. There are 142 volumes of elementary and secondary school textbooks, mainly for the years 1912-1950. The entire program is a relatively new one, and consequently only collections acquired in the past five years are adequate to support advanced studies.

Nearly two hundred titles are available at Library of Congress. The largest group (77 works) consists of histories, addresses, essays, lectures, and studies on adult education and regional development. The Ministry of Education is represented by its Boletim, Anais, Relatório, and miscellaneous publications; the Serviço de Estatística de Educação by various statistical compilations. Although state bulletins and reports match federal publications in quantity, they represent only the more important states. A limited amount of material (usually catalogs, circulars, and reports) is present for the following institutions of higher education: universities of Brazil and Sao Paulo, the catholic universities of Sao Paulo and Rio Grande do Sul, Instituto MacKenzie; similar items are present for a few colégios in Belém, Curitiba, Florianópolis, Rio de Janeiro, Salvador, and Sao Paulo. For the elementary level there are compilations of school laws and legislation.

The published bibliography (72) of the Pan American Union's holdings on adult education lists about seventy-five books, pamphlets, and articles pertaining to Brazil and covering the period from 1919 through the 1940's. In addition to general studies one finds works on adult literacy, use of audio-visual materials, agricultural and technical education and the educational role of libraries and museums. Some deal with individual states (e. g., Alagoas, Minas Gerais, Sao Paulo, and Sergipe). There are several pamphlets issued by the National Education Crusade in the 1930's and by the National Institute of Pedagogical Studies. Strength in educational journal holdings is indicated by the fact that for all but two of the titles mentioned below the collection is complete or nearly so.

Yale's holdings (about forty titles) consist mainly of official publications from the Ministry of Education, although some histories and monographic works and a number of publications from universities in Rio de Janeiro, Sao Paulo, and Curitiba are present.

Texas (97, 102) reports that resources for education are not a special feature of its Latin American collection and only those pertaining to one country (Mexico) are adequate for research. However, in the past two years it accessioned twenty-seven titles on Brazilian education, including some from the universities of Ceará, Recife, and Rio Grande do Sul. There has been little interest in developing this area at Illinois and Tulane.

Eleven libraries hold the Bibliografia Brasileira de Educação (P7) (1954-), but it is complete at Library of Congress and and Pan American Union. More widely held is Revista Brasileira de Estudos Pedagógicos (P55) (1944-) with full sets at California (Berkeley), Library of Congress, Pan American Union, and Texas--and some volumes at eleven other libraries. Most other journals are reported by three to six libraries: Educação (P36) (1940-) with best holdings at California (Berkeley), Educação e Ciências Sociais (P37) (1956-) and MEC (P46) (1956-) with complete sets only at Pan American Union, Revista da Campanha Nacional de Educação Rural (P63) (1954-) and Revista do Ensino (P74) (1951-) with Florida having the most nearly complete

holdings. Apparently only two institutions, Florida and Library
of Congress, have <u>EBSA: Documentário de Ensino</u> (P34) (1947?-)
but neither file is complete; only the latter receives <u>Revista do
Professor</u> (P84) (1941?-), which it does not retain permanently.
There are six subscriptions to <u>CAPES: Boletim Informativo da
Campanha Nacional de Aperfeiçoamento de Pessoal de Nível
Superior</u> (P25) (1952-), nearly all complete from volume one.
Two university reviews--<u>Anais da Universidade do Brasil</u> (P2)
(1950-) and <u>Kriterion</u>(P44) (1947-)--are widely held, while two
--<u>Revista da Universidade Católica de Campinas</u> (P66) (1954-)
and <u>Revista da Universidade Católica de São Paulo</u> (P67) (1952-)--
are not. Only Library of Congress and New York Public hold all
four (although not complete); most libraries (e.g., Florida, Harvard, Texas, Wisconsin, and Yale) report lacunae for the early
years of <u>Kriterion</u>.

ECONOMICS AND BUSINESS

For this field institutions report a considerable and growing
interest. One of the major parts of the Hull Collection at Cornell
(87) consists of a number of general works describing Brazil's
six economic cycles, each represented by a raw material: dye
wood, sugar, gold, cotton, coffee, and rubber. In general, Cornell rates its holdings of nineteenth century material adequate and
of publications of the last ten years very good; there are, for
instance, eighty volumes classified as economic history and fifty-
seven as commerce.

Resources at Texas (97, 102) in this field are outstanding
and include bank reports for the postwar period and many recent
publications as indicated by 121 accessions in the past two years,
representing such diverse aspects as economic history and development, foreign investment, economic conditions in various
regions and in specific states, agrarian reform, and laws affecting
business.

Holdings at Library of Congress are very extensive with
more than 1,200 titles in the classified collection. Approximately
five hundred works deal with economic conditions of the country
and its regions and states (especially the Amazon Valley, the
Northeast, Sao Paulo, and Rio Grande do Sul). Of current interest
are the planning and development reports of the Conselho do De-
senvolvimento and United States agencies having economic relations with Brazil--e.g., U.S. Tariff Commission, U.S. Technical
Mission to Brazil, and Agency for International Development (AID).
Some seventy works cover the economic aspects of agriculture,

including agricultural history, agricultural law and land tenure;
holdings on industry are smaller, but there are about fifty titles
on labor, laboring classes, social security, and labor laws.

Works classified as Commerce and Finance number about
five hundred titles--general works, commercial law and policy,
trade (foreign, coastwise and that of individual states). There
are bank statistics, reports of the Banco do Brasil and others,
the annual reports of the Rio de Janeiro and Sao Paulo stock ex-
changes, and a dozen works on insurance. Over 250 titles are
devoted to Public Finance; this section includes works on taxation
and studies of specific taxes--e.g., thirty-two books on income
tax, published as early as 1930. The collection contains over
one hundred items on transportation and communication, about a
third devoted to railroads. Here one finds several early items:
DeMoray's Report on the Proposed Railway in the Province of
Pernambuco, Brazil (1855), Gonçalves de Carvalho's A Estrada
de Ferro para Matto-Grosso e Bolivia (1876) and Branner's Railways of Brazil (1887). Fewer volumes relate to water transportation, merchant marine, street railways, air transport, and tele-
graph and telephone service.

Yale's resources amount to approximately three hundred
titles; about one third consists of general material published since
1900. Approximately sixty deal with the economic aspects of agriculture (with emphasis on coffee production) and an equal number
with commerce. In the transportation section one finds a few
early railroad annual reports, a complete file of the Brazilian
Traction Light and Power Company annual reports and broken runs
of those for the Rio de Janeiro and Sao Paulo Tramway Light and
Power companies. Florida's collection (over 300 titles) covers
economic history, commerce and industry, migration, land tenure and reform.

The Business Library at Columbia emphasizes government
documents and statistical information in this area; it receives
some material on exchange through the Federal Reserve Bank of
New York. Most of the titles in the Business Information Division
of the Cleveland Public appeared in the last twenty years; only a
few date from the 1920's and 1930's. Illinois had followed a selective acquisitions program for about twenty years, until assignment
of Brazil under the Farmington Plan brought responsibility for
collecting on a more comprehensive basis.

There is evidence of library specialization in certain aspects
of the broad field of economics and business. The Oliveira Lima
Library reports sizeable holdings on the history of economics; in

this area the James Ford Bell Collection at Minnesota contains substantial holdings on European commercial enterprises in Brazil prior to 1800, including a large amount of pamphlet material on the Dutch West India Co. Pennsylvania is strong in material relating to economic development in the twentieth century, while California (Berkeley) has recently given special attention to literature dealing with the economic development of the Northeast. Indiana has concentrated on contemporary economic conditions; the University Library houses forty volumes, exclusive of periodicals, government reports, and the like, while the Department of International Business Administration holds between eight hundred and nine hundred uncataloged items, consisting of pamphlets, conference reports, government publications, and other ephemera. The National Agricultural Library's field of major interest includes agricultural economics and statistics of production, trade, consumption, and the like, of agricultural products. The Land Tenure Center at Wisconsin (125) is forming a special collection devoted to land tenure and reform and land economics. Material on Brazil at present amounts to over fifty books, nearly all of them published in the past ten years. Among the authors are Manuel Diegues Júnior, Francisco Julião, Darcy Ribeiro, and Paulo Schilling. A number of the studies deal with the problems of the Northeast. Approximately one hundred other items (reprints, theses, issues of journals, university and school bulletins, project proposals, speeches, and newspaper clippings) supplement the book resources. The general catalog at Wisconsin lists over one hundred titles on 'economic conditions and policy.

Over one hundred titles are available at Michigan, Northwestern, Oklahoma, and Virginia; holdings at Iowa, Joint University Libraries, Kansas, Louisiana, Minnesota (exclusive of the Bell Collection), Newberry, and Tulane are smaller. Harvard, New York Public (47) and New York University contain unspecified amounts of material, and most of Chicago's Brazilian resources in social sciences fall into this field.

Journal holdings are strong. In 1938 Pan American Union (77) reported fifty titles relating to economic subjects (embracing agriculture, commerce, banking, and transportation). Seventeen journals in economics, business and labor exhibit considerable variation in both number of subscriptions and the extent to which holdings are complete. For each of such titles as Boletim do Ministério do Trabalho, Indústria, e Comércio (P15) (nova fase, 1951-), Conjuntura Econômica (P28) (1954-), Revista Brasileira de Economia (P53) (1947-) and Revista Brasileira de Estatística (P54) (1940-) about thirty libraries report holdings;

however, ten institutions--California (Berkeley), Florida, Harvard, Joint University Libraries, Library of Congress, Pan American Union, Texas, Stanford, Wisconsin, and Yale--have complete or very long runs of all four. California (Berkeley), Library of Congress, New York Public, Pan American Union, and Stanford also have full sets of Sintese Política Econômica Social (P92) (1959-). More than fourteen libraries have acquired some volumes of Brazilian Business (P24) (1921-) and O Observador Econômico e Financeiro (P51) (1936-), but the only two nearly complete sets of the former are at Cleveland Public and Library of Congress and of the latter at Joint University Libraries and Pan American Union. However, Comércio Internacional (P27) (1951-) is available at more than twenty institutions--the majority of files starting with volume 1. American libraries appear to have achieved only limited coverage of other journals: only three --California (Berkeley), Library of Congress and Pan American Union--maintain current subscriptions to Revista de Finanças Públicas (P70) (1941-), but none has a complete back file; Library of Congress has a full set, and Texas lacks one issue, of Industriários (P42) (1948-); New York Public has the only complete file of Revista do Conselho Nacional de Economia (P73) (1952-), and Econômica Brasileira (P35) (1955-) and lacks only a few numbers of IDORT: Revista de Organização e Produtividade (P41) (1932-); Pan American Union has acquired the only full sets of Mensagem Econômica (P47) (1952-) and Revista do Trabalho (P86) (1933-); and Library of Congress holds the best files of Digesto Econômico (P33) (1944-)and Revista do I. R. B. (P75) (1940-), although in each case some years are incomplete.

POLITICAL SCIENCE

Several libraries have developed strong collections in the field of political science. Holdings at Illinois, according to one faculty member, rank among the best six in the country. It is not surprising to find significant resources in this area at Library of Congress: over 175 works classified as constitutional history, constitutional reform and federal-state relations; sixty-seven as executive branch, administration, civil service, officials, and the like; about fifty on political parties and elections; and approximately 150 on state and local government. Among the more unusual items are a number of nineteenth century Brazilian political pamphlets (85). New York Public (33) has a number of early editions of Brazilian constitutions, while Cornell reports ninety-four volumes on constitutional history and Northwestern, sixty-four on the executive branch. There are seventy titles classified as political science at Yale, forty at Michigan, and 138 with the subject heading "Brazil--Politics and Government" at Wisconsin.

Pan American Union and Southern California actively collect material on politics; Princeton and New York University have recently increased their acquisitions in this area. Tulane's resources cover chiefly the period since 1930. Three institutions reported holdings of political science and law together: over two hundred volumes each at Minnesota and Virginia and over one hundred at Ohio State.

Pan American Union's holdings (73) on public administration are strong, especially for the period since 1940. Resources of books, journal articles, pamphlets, and government publications come to over five hundred items. They deal with administrative planning and administrative law, management of government-owned utilities, finance and budgeting; for personnel administration one finds studies of job classification and numerous examples of federal and state laws and regulations for government employees. A large section on state and city administration contains many works on the Brazilian município and on various states, especially Sao Paulo. Well represented are publications of the Departamento Administrativo do Serviço Público, Fundação Getúlio Vargas and Instituto Brasileiro de Administração. Texas recently acquired a number of books on this subject.

In the area of foreign and international affairs works on foreign relations in Library of Congress include a number of diplomatic histories written by Brazilians and published in the past twenty-five years. Of nearly fifty works on foreign relations with various countries, eighteen deal with relations between Brazil and the United States. Some thirty titles are available on the Brazilian diplomatic service, including regulations, lists of diplomats and the like. The description published in 1933 of Duke's holdings (51) indicates the chief documentary sources held at that time; they embrace two Portuguese collections--Quadro elementar das Relações politicas e diplomaticas de Portugal (1842-1860) and Corpo diplomatico Portuguez contendo Actos e Relações politicos e diplomaticos de Portugal (1862-) (also present in Oliveira Lima Library) which contain much material on Brazil--Brazilian documentary sources and monographic works in French and English as well as Portuguese. Northwestern has twenty-eight works on Brazilian foreign relations.

Pan American Union (81) has a notable collection on inter-American relations, covering such topics as the conferences of the American states, the inter-American system, the Monroe Doctrine and relations of this country with individual nations like

Brazil. Southern California has actively collected on international relations for many years.

Among the journals in this field two, Revista Brasileira de
Política International (P59) (1958-) and Revista do Serviço Público (P85) (1937-), are very widely held. Of thirty-eight libraries reporting some volumes of the former, more than half
possess a complete set. In the case of the older journal, there
are lacunae in nearly all files, but one finds very substantial
runs at Duke, Florida, Harvard, Michigan, Pan American Union,
Pennsylvania, Stanford, Texas, Wisconsiń, and Yale. Revista
Brasileira de Estudos Políticos (P56) (1956-) enjoys wide distribution also with complete sets at California (Berkeley), Florida,
Michigan, Pennsylvania, Stanford, and Texas. In contrast,
only Pan American Union has the entire run of Revista Brasileira
dos Municípios (P60) (1948) and Revista de Administração Municipal (P68) (1954-), although other institutions hold some volumes.
Revista Interamericana do Ministério Público (P89) (1956-) is
available at Columbia, Florida, Harvard, Library of Congress,
New York Public, Pan American Union and Texas (generally
complete), but the best of the four reported sets of Estudos
Sociais (P38) (1958-) is found at Pan American Union.

LAW

A list of large foreign law collections in American law
libraries appeared in a recent article (92). They are, in descending order of size, Library of Congress, Harvard, Michigan,
Columbia, Yale, Los Angeles County Law Library, Association
of the Bar of New York, and Northwestern. The author points
out that Library of Congress and Harvard are the major research
collections for law in the world, because "they acquire material
for all jurisdictions, for all periods of time, for all aspects of
legal research." It is not surprising therefore to find extensive
holdings of Brazilian legal materials at both institutions.

The development of the Brazilian collection at Harvard (84)
dates back at least to 1913, when Dr. Walter Lichenstein spent
a year in the South American countries and assembled complete
or all but complete collections of their legislation, of the decisions of their courts and of their more important treaties. In 1925
a large collection of Brazilian legislation and decisions was added,
and holdings are now very substantial, occupying fifty-seven sections of shelving. Resources encompass a number of editions of
the various constitutions, the session laws from 1808, and recent
editions of codes. There are collections of the decisions of the

Supremo Tribunal and of other courts for the past fifty years or longer.

For the states (provinces prior to 1891) the Harvard Law Library in 1956 reported the following holdings (34); since then it has maintained the files indicated below as "to date," although it has not added any sets of laws or reports.

Acre: a few decisions only.

Alagoas: a compilation of laws, 1835-72. Session laws from 1888 to 1932. Decisions of the Tribunal Superior, 1904-10.

Amazonas: the constitution of 1935. Laws from 1852 to 1927. After 1927, session laws are published only in the Diario, which the library does not have. Decisions of the Tribunal Superior from 1894 to 1934.

Bahia: the constitutions of 1891 and 1935. Laws from 1901 to 1937. Reports of decisions 1894-1903 and 1932-34.

Ceará: laws from 1894 to 1938. No decisions.

Espírito Santo: five constitutions. Laws from 1899. Reports of the Tribunal Superior, 1920-25.

Federal District [i.e., Guanabara]: some procedural codes. Municipal laws, 1893-1921.

Goiás: three constitutions. Laws from 1892 to 1930.

Maranhão: laws from 1900. No decisions.

Minas Gerais: the constitutions of 1891 and 1936. Laws from 1891. Some procedural codes. Reports of decisions from 1904 as contained in Revista Forense.

Pará: the constitutions of 1891 and 1935. A few laws and reports of decisions.

Paraíba: the constitution of 1935. Some procedural codes. Laws from 1892. Decisions from 1907 as contained in Revista do Foro, 1907 to date.

Paraná: the constitutions of 1892 and 1935. A fairly complete collection of laws and decrees from 1890 (decretos to 1928, leis to 1929). Reports of decisions are contained in Paraná Judiciário, which the Library has.

Pernambuco: the constitutions of 1930 and 1935. Leis and decretos from 1924 to 1940, and a number of separate laws, as well as codes of procedure. Eight volumes of decisions.

Piauí: the constitutions of 1892 and 1935. Laws and decrees from 1889 to 1946.

Rio de Janeiro: laws and decrees from 1889 to 1912, but not complete. Decisions of the courts as contained in Relatório do Tribunal and Boletim Judiciário.

Rio Grande do Norte: the constitutions of 1907 and 1947. Actos Legislativos e Decretos (1889-1947), issued in two parts: Leis and Decretos.

Rio Grande do Sul: the constitutions of 1891, 1935, and 1947. Laws and decrees from 1890 to 1941. A few procedural codes. Reports and decisions as contained in Decisões do Superior Tribunal (1895-1928); also Revista Jurídica (1953 to date).

Santa Catarina: the constitution of 1935. Laws from 1835 to 1929. Reports of decisions as contained in Jurisprudencia do Superior Tribunal (1891-98, 1911-20, 1953 to date).

São Paulo: the constitutions of 1891 and 1935. Laws and decrees from 1892 to date. Reports of decisions as contained in Gazeta Jurídica (1893-1907), São Paulo Judiciário (1903-14) and Revista dos Tribunaes (1912 on).

São Pedro: very little.

Sergipe: the constitutions of 1901 and 1935. Laws and decrees from 1889 to 1924. Reports of decisions as contained in Sergipe Judiciário (1828-30).

The Brazilian collection in the Law Library of Library of Congress numbered 12,254 volumes in 1964, exclusive of periodicals and material in special collections (total holdings would probably have come to 20,000 volumes). Many of the earlier acquisitions figure in Borchard's Guide to the Law and Legal Literature of Argentina, Brazil and Chile (114), which now has limited value, because it appeared nearly fifty years ago; however, a supplement covering the period since 1917 is in preparation and will provide a much more accurate indication of present resources.

The following general description follows the arrangement of material on the shelves. There are fifty-six editions (including translations into English) of constitutions with publication dates as early as 1855, the session laws complete since 1808, and some fifty titles considered general collections of Brazilian law. Holdings of codes (civil, civil procedure, criminal, criminal procedure, and commercial) are strong and date from the mid-nineteenth century. Some five hundred special statutes and codes, arranged alphabetically by subject, cover such fields as accounting, administration, aeronautics, aliens, banking, bankruptcy, civil service, corporations, education, extradition, immigration, insurance, labor, land titles, leases, marriage, military law, mining, patents, petroleum, railroads, rent, social security, tariffs, and taxation. Although most imprints are post-1940, some carry earlier dates--a few from the nineteenth century. Court reports include Decisões do Governo da República dos Estados Unidos do Brasil (1826/28-1911)--decisions together with administrative matters; Annuario de Jurisprudência; Archivo Judiciário; and Revista do Supremo Tribunal. Over fifty digests deal with property, elections, workmen's compensation, and the like. The collection of monographs, many of them text-books, covers a wide range of subjects (e.g., philosophy of law, medical jurisprudence, contracts, taxation) and numbers over 2,000 titles.

For the states there is a great deal of material, but the Library has not always made systematic attempts to collect these items on a comprehensive basis. Holdings for Sao Paulo are undoubtedly the strongest and comprise the constitution of 1891, laws and decrees from 1892, decisions as found in Sao Paulo Judiciário and Revista dos Tribunaes, about twenty treatises and some individual laws. Ample material has also been gathered for Rio Grande do Sul. Substantial runs of the laws and decisions of Bahia, Ceará, Maranhão, Minas Gerais, Pará, Paraná, Pernambuco, Santa Catarina, and Sergipe are present, in contrast to relatively little for Alagoas, Espírito Santo, Goiás, Guanabara,

Mato Grosso, Paraíba, Piauí, and Rio Grande do Norte. One finds little on cities--only a few scattered items for Belém, Curitiba, Fortaleza and, of course, Sao Paulo, because this type of material is classified in the Library's general collections.

Serial publications constitute one of the truly notable features of these resources, not only in number of titles present but also in the fact that a very high percentage of them are complete from the first volume. In addition to general journals, there are periodicals published by various legal associations (e.g., Associação dos Advogados de Sao Paulo, Instituto da Ordem dos Advogados Brasileiros, Sociedade Brasileira de Direito Internacional); for special topics (Revista Brasileira de Direito Aeronáutico, Revista de Direito Mercantil, Revista Brasileira de Criminologia e Direito Penal, Revista de Direito Comercial, Revista de Direito Rodoviário, Revista de Direito Público e de Administração Federal, Revista Imposto da Renda) and by the law faculties of the various universities (Sao Paulo, Rio Grande do Sul, MacKenzie, Minas Gerais, Paraná, Bahia, Recife, and Ceará).

Florida's approximately one thousand volumes of legal material emphasize the twentieth century and embrace legal treatises, current legislation, codes, and reports. Gathered by Professor William D. Macdonald, the collection provides material for research in family property law.

Columbia (21) has designated only Argentina and Brazil among the Latin American republics for comprehensive coverage of legal material. At present the Law Library holds about 850 titles, including constitutions, court reports, session laws, serials, and treatises on comparative law. Noteworthy series include Jurisprudência. Supremo Tribunal Federal; O Direito; Revista do Direito Civil, Commercial e Criminal; Revista de Jurisprudência Brasileira; and Revista do Supremo Tribunal Federal. There is a special collection on boundary questions among the various South American countries. At Duke (51) one finds material relating to the northern boundary of Brazil with France and to the southern with Argentina; several items printed in as few as thirty copies are available. Duke also owns other legal material. There are extensive holdings of official and unofficial publications on questions of the boundaries of Brazil with Peru, French and British Guiana, and Argentina at Texas (97). The Library also has a complete file of the laws of Brazil, 1833-1913, and continues to develop its legal holdings. Michigan (8) also has acquired significant holdings of Brazilian law; the collection now amounts to about 850 volumes.

Northwestern's Law Library (70) contains over six hundred volumes of Brazilian publications, including recent editions of the most important codes and a number of commentaries. As examples of the fourteen periodicals one might cite Revista de Direito Civil (vols. 1-108, 1906-1933), Revista Brasileira de Direito Aeronáutico (vol. 1- ; 1955-), Revista da Faculdade de Direito, Universidade de São Paulo (vol. 26- ; 1930-), and Revista Forense (vol. 81- ; 1940-).

New York Public (9, 86) has complete files of the session laws of Brazil and in 1962 acquired a group of twelve Portuguese and Brazilian laws dated from 1748 to 1770. Printed in Lisbon, they deal with administrative and financial aspects of the government of the colony. In 1933 the Oliveira Lima Library at Catholic University (54) contained over two hundred volumes of laws and codes of Brazil.

Although resources of Brazilian law at Wisconsin are not strong, the Law Library recently acquired forty-five titles of codes, commentaries, and treatises that bear on the question of land reform. In contrast with its political science holdings, Illinois rates its resources in law as weak.

For serial publications little information is available. Only three Brazilian titles--Direito, Revista da Faculdade de Direito, Universidade de São Paulo, and Revista Forense--are among the 263 periodicals indexed in the Index to Foreign Legal Periodicals (91). In 1961 the following libraries subscribed to all of them: Columbia, Harvard, Library of Congress, Los Angeles County Law Library, Michigan, and Yale. In the District of Columbia, aside from Library of Congress, some titles are available at Pan American Union and other law libraries (43, 82).

GEOGRAPHY, TRAVEL, AND MAPS

There are a number of libraries with special holdings in this field, chiefly the accounts of early voyages of discovery and exploration (58). For the larger collections of this type it is of course impossible to do more than suggest the extent of such resources by naming a few representative examples.

Texas (69, 97) possesses one of the largest and richest collections. It includes reprints of the early chronicles of Brazil (e.g., the Diario of Pero Lopes de Sousa, the Warhafftige... Beschreibung of Ulrich Schmidel), of letters and reports of Jesuits who worked in the Amazon basin and reports of travelers, such as Johann Baptist von Spix and Karl Friedrich Philipp von Martius. There is a total of over nine hundred volumes; recent additions cover general geographical works, the geography of regions (e. g. , Rio Grande do Sul, the Amazon) and specific studies such as numerous books on Brasília. Publications in French and German are represented in the collection as well as those in Portuguese and English.

In the Hull Collection at Cornell (87) there are a number of sixteenth century works of travel and exploration--e. g. , Montalboddo's Paesi novamente ritrovati (1517) and Itinerarium Portugallensium (1508), Thevet's The New Found Worlde (1568), Lery's Histoire d'un voyage fait en la terre du Bresil, autrement dite Amerique (1594), Ulrich Schmidel's Vera historia (1599). Later publications include the rare Nuevo descubrimiento del gran rio de las Amazonas (1641) of Acuña, the rare 1647 edition of Baerle's Rerum per octennium in Brasilia, and there are also many nineteenth century travel books. In all, Cornell reports 350 volumes classified as description and travel.

Likewise famous for early travel accounts is the Oliveira Lima Library at Catholic University (14). There are fine copies of the first and second French books on Brazil (Thevet's Singularitez and Lery's Histoire), Acuña's Nuevo descubrimiento and Johan Nieuhoff's Gedenkweerdige brasiliaense Zee-en Lantreize in both Dutch and English editions. With over six hundred volumes (exclusive of Jesuit relations) the Library is, in general, very rich in travel literature of all periods.

At Newberry there is a fine group of books of travel in the general resources, while the Ayer Collection holds many important works on the great voyages of discovery and exploration. The total exceeds two hundred accounts and does include (in contrast to the Library's general emphasis on the colonial period) a number of nineteenth and twentieth century works. Here too appear Thevet and Staden for the sixteenth century; Acuña and Vasconcellos' Chronica da Companhia de Jesu do estado do Brasil for the seventeenth; John Black, Authentic narrative... (1798), Marques Pereira, Compendio narrativo do peregrino da America (1731),and Philadelphia Stevens, Briefe über Portugal...Brasilien (1782) for the eighteenth. There are numerous titles for the past 150 years.

Minnesota holds approximately 190 titles in this field, about 60 per cent of general travel and exploration, 15 per cent more specialized, and 25 per cent on the Amazon River basin. One-

half of the titles are in English, with the remainder chiefly in
Portuguese, Spanish, and French. Literature of early exploration and travel forms the bulk of the holdings. In addition, the
Library's James Ford Bell Collection contains substantial resources relating to Brazil, although they are limited to the period prior to 1800. Beginning with the accounts of the earliest
Portuguese voyages along the Brazilian coast and with the portolan charts showing the place names given by the Portuguese, the
collection follows the growth of Portuguese enterprise in Brazil.
The earliest editions of the French works by Lery, Thevet,
Abbeville, and others are present as well as sixteenth and seventeenth century writings by Hans Staden, Ulrich Schmidel, Johan
Nieuhoff, and Kaspar van Baerle.

The Bernardo Mendel collection recently acquired by Indiana contains over 230 volumes relating directly to Brazil. They
extend from the first printed reference to a Portuguese voyage
to Brazil (Copia der Newen Eytung aus Presilg Landt, 1514/15)
through the early editions of the Vespucci letters and the Montalboddo compilation of voyages into sixteenth and seventeenth century items. The sizeable collection of early voyages and travels
at Kansas includes a number of similar items--e.g., Purchas
His Pilgrimes, 1625-1626 (the fourth edition with the fifth volume
supplement), Theodor de Bry's Reisen im occiden talischen In-
dien, 1590-1630 and Thevet's Historia (1561). Kentucky has
gathered a few books from the sixteenth through eighteenth centuries on the discovery and exploration of Brazil (e.g., Baerle),
but its holdings are uneven and have developed in haphazard
rather than systematic fashion. A number of early works, together with a long series of later travel books, is also found in
the Branner Collection at Stanford. The Hispanic Society of
America (36-38) has a published catalog to consult. Nearly half
of the approximately one hundred entries for travel works listed
there are for publications issued before 1821, and it must be remembered that there are separate catalogs for works published
prior to 1700.

Among the early works at Library of Congress (34) is the
letter which Amerigo Vespucci wrote to Lorenzo de Medici about
the results of his third voyage to the continent (during which he
explored the east coast of Brazil) that was later to bear his name.
Of the thirteen editions in Latin printed between 1503 and 1506,
Library of Congress has two, the second issue of the third edition,
entitled Mundus novus (1504), and the sixth entitled De ora Ant-
arctica (1505). Also present are Hans Staden, Acuña, Baerle
(four editions, including the rare 1647), nine editions of Lery's
Histoire, and various works of the seventeenth and eighteenth

centuries, as well as numerous accounts written by Americans and British who visited Brazil in the nineteenth century. Of association interest is the copy of President Theodore Roosevelt's Through the Brazilian Wilderness from his Hunting Library and the copy of Pereira da Cunha's Viagens e caçadas em Matto Grosso (1918) presented to the President. The collection of general description and travel approaches six hundred titles, divided chronologically into four groups.

TABLE V

WORKS OF DESCRIPTION AND TRAVEL
IN LIBRARY OF CONGRESS, BY PERIOD

Period	Number of Titles
Early to 1821	88
1822 - 1889	167
1890 - 1950	272
1951 to date	47
TOTAL	574

NOTE: Excludes books classified with regions and states, cities and towns.
SOURCE: Derived from shelf list (F 2511-2516), Library of Congress.

The published catalog (66) of New York Public's holdings in the history of Americas provides a listing of that institution's unusual strength in this field. Of works of description and travel about Brazil there are over six hundred titles, with about one-third prior to 1800, one-third for the nineteenth century, and the remainder for the period from 1900 to date. Works by Baerle, Acuña, and Lery figure among the more unusual items.

Publications of nineteenth century English-speaking travelers in Brazil seem, in general, to be readily available in American libraries. A list* of twenty-two accounts by Louis Agassiz,

*Charles Granville Hamilton, "English Speaking Travelers in Brazil, 1851-1887," Hispanic American Historical Review, XL (1960), 533-547.

Richard F. Burton, William Lewis Herndon, D.P. Kidder, and others, was checked with the National Union Catalog for locations. Of these titles published between 1851 and 1887 only four were held by five or fewer libraries; sixteen by between nine and twenty institutions; and the other two by more than twenty libraries. Library of Congress owns 20, Catholic University and New York Public 14 each, Princeton 12, American Antiquarian Society, Cleveland Public and Library Company of Philadelphia 11 each, California (Berkeley) and Duke 9 each.

The Joint University Libraries have about 475 titles in geography and travel. The acquisition policy emphasizes the sources provided by accounts of Brazilian and foreign travelers. The principal writers from the United States, England, France, and Germany are all present, and holdings show strength in regional travels and reports on such special aspects as the German and Italian colonies in southern Brazil. The collection of works by Brazilians themselves is increasing.

Although most of Yale's holdings (about 350 titles) treat the country as a whole, more than fifty devoted to the Amazon region form an interesting group. The two earliest titles are Acuña's Nuevo descubrimiento (1641) and the English translation of Blaise François de Pagan's Historical and Geographical Description of the Great Country and River of the Amazones (1661). There are also some nineteenth century works, but the majority consist of American and British publications issued since 1900. Two unusual items are volumes of photographs of Belém, one from the nineteenth century and one from 1902. One finds lesser amounts of material devoted to Rio de Janeiro and Sao Paulo, but the collection lacks any other regional emphasis.

Although the resources at Duke (51)--as reported in 1933-- do not contain a great many early editions, the Library has made a special effort to assemble travel books covering the period since 1822. Among them one finds a number of accounts on the Amazon basin (e.g., those by Sir Richard Burton and Franz Keller) and numerous works of a descriptive nature covering either the country as a whole or particular states or regions (e.g., Pará, Bahia, Minas Gerais).

Pan American Union (27, 75) holds Baerle's Rerum per octennium in Brasilia in the 1647 edition and the Piso-Marggraf Historia naturalis Brasiliae (1648), as well as numerous modern works on Brazilian geography. Florida's resources (313 titles) are strongest in cultural geography and travel material. American Geographical Society (1) has extensive holdings of geograph-

ical material. Only statistics of other libraries' holdings are
available: Illinois 900 volumes; Virginia 300; Northwestern 230;
Ohio State 150; Tulane 140 (chiefly twentieth century in coverage);
Harvard's collection in geography is included in 1,500 volumes
covering that subject, economic conditions and local history.
The following reported in terms of titles rather than volumes:
Pennsylvania 244; Louisiana 148; Wisconsin 142; and Washington
(Seattle) 75.

In atlases and maps Library of Congress also possesses
outstanding resources. Thirty-eight Brazilian atlases range in
time from the Atlas do Imperio do Brazil (1868) to the Conselho
Nacional de Geografia's Atlas do Brasil (1959), although most
have appeared since the turn of the century; also held are atlases
prepared for the states of Bahia, Espírito Santo, Minas Gerais,
Paraná, Rio de Janeiro, and Santa Catarina. In addition, the
index to the published catalog (117) shows that many general atlases in the collection contain maps of Brazil. The Mendel Collection at Indiana contains many classic sixteenth and seventeenth
century atlases, and a number of Brazilian atlases are available
at Chicago, John Crear, and Newberry (16).

Library of Congress (116) has assembled probably the best
general collection of Brazilian maps in the United States. Its
acquisition policy embraces all official maps, commercial city
plans, road, and special maps; the Map Division's annual report
has frequently mentioned receiving more than one hundred maps
from Brazil during the year. Holdings fall into several groups:
six hundred general maps (i.e., showing the entire country or
large parts of it), including about one hundred from the seventeenth through nineteenth centuries. Seventeen manuscript maps,
dating from the latter part of the eighteenth century, deal with
the boundaries between the Spanish and Portuguese colonial pos-
sessions (55). Nine relate to the southwestern boundary of Brazil,
and the remainder to the northwestern. Six of the former, made
by order of the Spanish commissioner, carry his signature, Josef
Varela y Ulloa; those in the northwestern group, all by Francisco
Requena and dated from August 1788 to January 1789, cover the
Amazon and Japurá Rivers.

About nine hundred subject maps depict physical features,
economic aspects, agriculture, mines and minerals, transportation and communication, and the like. Although regions and
natural features (e.g., rivers, mountains, the São Francisco
River and basin) make up a small group of sixty items, an equal
number (filed under South America rather than Brazil) deal with
the Amazon Valley, of which the largest number date from the

early years of this century. Of approximately 5,700 maps of
states, holdings for Sao Paulo are most extensive (about 1,000
items) with Bahia, Minas Gerais, and Rio Grande do Sul also
well represented. About one-half of the state maps consist of
single maps of the municípios, many of them using medium scale
(1:150,000) and containing insets of the important cities. Street
maps and city plans comprise the bulk of the 1,000 city maps.
There are many for Sao Paulo and relatively few for other cities.

Other map resources include topographic series and sets,
many of which have not yet been completed by the issuing agency.
Sheets for coastal and some interior areas are available in the
1:500,000 Carta do Brasil of the Conselho Nacional de Geografia;
a 1:100,000 set for the state of Minas Gerais is nearly 80 per
cent complete, and there are large scale (1:5,000) maps of both
Rio de Janeiro and Sao Paulo.

The Ayer Collection at Newberry contains some maps of
Brazil or some section of her coasts. A beautiful and important
example is Manuscript Map No. 26, a portolan atlas attributed
by the late Armando Cortesão to the master Portuguese cartog-
rapher Sebastião Lopes (ca. 1565).

The Map Division of New York Public owns a number of
maps of Brazil (some being photocopies), dated from 1568 to the
present. The Manuel E. Gondra Collection at Texas (13) includes
270 maps, atlases, and charts (originals, drafts, copies, blue-
prints, tracings, and printed pieces). Of these eighteen maps
are of Brazil and one of Sao Paulo. There are about four hundred
maps at Illinois, between 200 and 250 at Indiana, and forty at
Minnesota. New York University, Ohio State, Pan American
Union (80),and Syracuse also have holdings of this form of material,. but California (Berkeley) reports that its map collection is
only average.

A rather uneven distribution characterizes journal subscriptions in this field. Complete sets of the two publications of the
Conselho Nacional de Geografia, Revista Brasileira de Geografia
(P58) (1939-) and Boletim Geográfico (P18) (1943-), are available at California (Berkeley), Harvard, Joint University Libraries,
Louisiana, Northwestern, Pan American Union, and Wisconsin,
with many additional institutions holding the former and a considerable number the latter. Florida, Library of Congress, and
Wisconsin report all volumes of the Revista Geográfica (P88)
(1941-) of the Pan American Institute of Geography and History,
while apparently only California (Berkeley) and Harvard have
maintained a full run of the long established Revista da Sociedade

Brasileira de Geografia (P65) (1885-), although Library of
Congress, Michigan, and New York Public lack relatively few
issues. The three publications of the Associação dos Geógrafos
Brasileiros are not present in many libraries; the Anais (P1)
(1949-) is complete only at Miami and Pan American Union,
Boletim Paulista de Geografia (P20) (1949-) at California
(Berkeley), Duke, Harvard, Pan American Union, Stanford,and
Texas, but only five libraries report Boletim Carioca de Geografia
(P10) (1950-)   with California (Berkeley), Illinois, and Wiscon-
sin possessing nearly complete files.

HISTORY

        History, like literature, constitutes a field of special
interest to American libraries. Not only are such collections as
the Oliveira Lima (Catholic University), Hull (Cornell), Greenlee
(Newberry), and Branner (Stanford) conspicuous by their strength
in this subject, but acquisition policies of other libraries have
also emphasized it. In view of this, it is surprising to find relatively little specific information available about these resources.
As an exception we do have the detailed bibliographic essay on
Duke's collection (51), which devotes a great deal of attention to
history; although published in 1933, it makes a good starting point.

        Duke's holdings (in history, political science, and geography
they now total approximately 4, 100 volumes) are strong in their
documentary character and contemporary source material. Early
in the colonial period appeared descriptive and historical works
dealing with a sufficiently large portion of Brazil to be considered general rather than sectional in nature. The Library has
Roteiro Geral com largas informações de toda a costa do Brazil
(1587), by Gabriel Soares de Sousa, second noted historian of
Brazil, and works of other colonial writers (e.g., Frei Vicente
do Salvador, Sebastião da Rocha Pitta, Antonio de Santa Maria
Jaboatão), though not always in the first edition. The Library
contains, in addition, material dealing with the various captain-
cies (Maranhão, Pernambuco, Bahia, Rio de Janeiro, and
others); the large amount of material available for Sao Paulo includes such collections of unedited material as Documentos Inte-
ressantes para a historia de São Paulo, Documentos Historicos
Providoria da Fazenda Real de Santos, and Actas da Camara da
Villa de S. Paulo. For the national period the Library has made
special efforts to obtain the collections of public documents, as
well as an adequate number of general histories written sinece
1822 (e.g., those by João Capistrano de Abreu, José Francisco
da Rocha Pombo, Manoel de Oliveira Lima). There are a number

of works dealing with individual states and regions; examples of
the more unusual include José Antonio Marinho's Historia do
Movimento politico que no Anno de 1842 teve Lugar na Provincia
de Minas Gerais, Revista do Instituto Archeologico e Geographi-
co Pernambuco, and Revista do Archivo Publico do Rio Grande
do Sul.

The Oliveira Lima Collection at Catholic University (14, 54)
contains several thousand volumes dealing either directly or indirectly with every period of Brazilian history and culture in
general, many of them in original editions unavailable elsewhere
in this country. The standard works of the majority of Brazilian
historians are therefore to be found as a matter of course, but
there are also less important collateral texts little known outside
of Brazil and records from archives of various states and munici-
palities. A special feature of the collection consists of rare
Dutch tracts and books relating to the Dutch occupation of Pernambuco in the seventeenth century. There are groups of pamphlets
on the Dutch military exploits around Olinda and on the Dutch
West India Co. By way of contrast, also present are Portuguese
accounts of the Dutch occupation of the area.

Newberry's holdings are concentrated in two special groups:
the Ayer Collection and the Greenlee Collection. In both cases
the colonial period has received emphasis. Some of the notable
items among approximately four hundred titles are long runs of
the publications of documents in the various Brazilian archives.
Since the publication of the printed catalog of the Greenlee Collection (67), containing 1,291 entries under Brazil, resources have
increased greatly. Within the collection political, ecclesiastical,
social, cultural, economic, military and local history figure as
important subdivisions. A few examples of notable items are
Brito Freire, Nova Lusitania (1675), Santa Thereza, Istoria delle
guerre del Regno del Brasile (1698), and José da Silva Lisboa,
Synopse da legislação principal do senhor D. João VI (1818).

Holdings of the New York Public (9, 66) are excellent for
Brazilian history, in both quantity and quality of materials. Periodical sets include those which reprint documents and archives
extensively, those devoted to historical commentary and those
concerned with contemporary affairs. The Library has attempted
to collect comprehensively material relating to international
questions. The catalog of the history of Americas with about
seven hundred entries under "Brazil--History" provides some indication of the strength and scope of the collection.

It is difficult to assess the resources in history at Library of Congress, but among Brazilian holdings they rank second only to literature in extent. General materials include ninety-seven titles classified as periodicals, societies, collections, 106 as general biography and genealogy, fourteen as historiography, and about two hundred as general historical treatises.

Turning to different periods, one finds over 1,200 titles distributed among five epochs.

TABLE VI

BRAZILIAN HISTORY IN LIBRARY OF CONGRESS,
BY PERIOD

Period	Number of Titles
1500 - 1548	33
1549 - 1762	215
1763 - 1821	34
1822 - 1889	376
1890 to date	561
TOTAL	1,219

SOURCE: Derived from shelf list (F 2526-2538.2), Library of Congress.

Some emphases and special features deserve comment. There is a group of twenty-two titles by and about Hans Staden, including the 1557 edition of his Wahrhaftige Historia and several other early editions. Among the one hundred works dealing with the Dutch conquest are about twenty contemporary pamphlets printed in Amsterdam, the Hague, and elsewhere. Eighteenth century holdings contain several biographies of Tiradentes, leader of the Inconfidência Mineira, and nineteenth century material eleven biographies of the Duque de Caxias. For later figures there are 34 works by and about Joaquim Nabuco, 75 by and about Rui Barbosa, 25 by and about Rio Branco, and 55 by and about Getúlio Vargas. Among the 136 titles on the Paraguayan War (classified with Paraguayan History) would be material on Brazil's participation.

Approximately 1,400 titles deal with state and local history, with special strength on the Amazon Valley--its history, Indians, flora and fauna, and the like. There are 155 titles on the state of Sao Paulo, 130 on the city of Rio de Janeiro, 108 on Rio Grande do Sul, 76 on Minas Gerais, 72 on Pernambuco, 60 on Bahia, 56 on Pará, 55 on the city of Sao Paulo, 55 on Mato Grosso, and 47 on Paraná.

Another strong collection can be found at Texas (97). To its over 2,400 volumes additions are constantly being made. It contains reprints of early chronicles, the histories of the early period (e.g., by Alphonse de Beauchamp and Robert Southey) and those by such later writers as Joaquim Nabuco and Oliveira Lima.

With two special collections Cornell's resources (87) are also notable. In 1895 the University acquired the books of Herbert H. Smith (the majority of them bought during his eight year residence in Brazil); the 1,500 volumes embraced most of the nineteenth century publications on the country. A half-century later the University received as a gift the private library of Francis R. Hull--with its wealth of material on all phases of Brazilian life. Extensive purchases of serials in the last ten years have further strengthened resources, which now include over 1,100 volumes classified as history, divided as follows: periodicals, societies, and the like, 281; general and chronological 450; and local history 410.

The Yale Library contains approximately five hundred titles dealing with Brazilian history. Material is distributed over the various periods, but several twentieth century items deserve mention: a book of mounted clippings on Brazil, taken from newspapers from November 26, 1907 to December 31, 1908 and collected by Hiram Bingham; approximately thirty works by and about Vargas and his régime; and a compilation of documents on the proposal for Operación Panamericana, issued between 1958 and 1960 by the Serviço de Documentação of the Presidência. For local history the Amazon region and the state of Sao Paulo are best represented.

Harvard reports that its resources amount to five hundred volumes of general history, 1,200 of history by period, and 1,500 of economic conditions, local history, and geography, in addition to 1,000 volumes of Brazilian periodicals. At the Joint University Libraries there are about six hundred titles classified as Brazilian history, including sets of the principal historical reviews and collections. Publications of the Arquivo Municipal for such cities as Curitiba, Sao Paulo, Porto Alegre, and Bahia

make the collection good in regional material. Wisconsin's resources on the history and geography of Brazil amount to about
1,500 volumes (excluding serials). Of seventy-three entries
under Brazil in the Guide to Historical Literature, forty-four are
present in the Library's collection; distribution over the various
periods is even; all but one of the bibliographies are owned, but
most of the items listed under "Archival Collections" have not
been acquired.

A collection of Portuguese Africa material recently pur-
chased by Florida bears indirectly on Brazil, and there are plans
to expand holdings on slavery and the slave trade. At the present
time material on Brazilian history (259 titles) provides general
coverage for all periods. A notable holding is Brito Freire's
Nova Lusitania (1675).

Other libraries' resources are mentioned more briefly below. The American Antiquarian Society has 250 volumes on the
history and description of Brazil; holdings are strong in early
standard works now difficult to obtain. The George Early Church
Collection on Latin America at Brown contains some material on
Brazil. Holdings at California (Berkeley) are better for the
colonial period and for southern Brazil than for the national
period and other regions. California (Los Angeles) rates its resources as a sound basic collection which needs additional development. Practically all standard works are found in the Branner
Collection at Stanford; in addition, it contains the most important
books dealing with the Dutch occupation. Cleveland Public has
limited its holdings of Brazilian history, because another library
accepted responsibility for that country in a cooperative program
for acquisitions among libraries in the area; nevertheless, several hundred volumes are available. The Hispanic Society (36) has,
as for other subjects, concentrated on the colonial period; the
published catalog contains over one hundred entries under "Brazil
--History." Nineteenth and twentieth century publications comprise most of Illinois's six hundred volumes and of Iowa's 175
titles (of which twenty-eight deal with the Amazon River and
valley).

Statistics for other libraries include the following: 500 titles
at Pennsylvania (the collection is stronger in the national than in
the colonial period);   220 at Minnesota;   129 at Louisiana; 100
at Washington (Seattle) and the same number at Washington (St.
Louis).   There are 750 volumes at Princeton; 582 at Northwestern;
500 at Virginia; 250 at Kansas; 200 at Ohio State; and 100 at Oklahoma (including politics and law).

New Mexico's holdings in history and geography approximate 2,500 volumes and Michigan's, 800 titles. Indiana reports four hundred volumes on history and government, with most standard works present and particular strength in the colonial period. New York University and Missouri report history as one of the important subjects in their Brazilian holdings, and it is one of the strong fields at Pan American Union.

Most persons would rate Revista do Instituto Histórico e Geográfico Brasileiro (P78) (1839-) the most important journal in the field. Complete sets were reported by eight libraries-- California (Berkeley) Cleveland Public, Hispanic Society, Newberry, Pan American Union, Stanford, Texas, and Wisconsin-- and substantially complete by Harvard, Michigan, Princeton, and Yale. California (Berkeley), Duke, Joint University Libraries, and Newberry possess all volumes of Revista do Instituto Histórico e Geográfico de São Paulo (P79) (1895-), as do eleven institutions--California (Berkeley), Duke, Florida, Harvard, New Mexico, New York Public, Pan American Union, Pennsylvania, Stanford, Texas, and Yale--of Revista de História (P71) (1950-). Apparently there are only three full sets--at Miami, Pan American Union, and Wisconsin--of Revista do Museu Júlio de Castilhos e Arquivo Histórico do Rio Grande do Sul. California (Berkeley) and New York Public, among thirteen institutions, have complete files of Anais do Museu Histórico Nacional (P3) (1940-).

Science and Technology

5

GENERAL

It is much more difficult to assess American libraries'
holdings of Brazilian works in science and technology than in
other fields. Because such material cannot be so readily identified in relation to a country or region, few libraries reported on
specific resources. The fact that the bulk of science literature
is serial in form poses special problems. Moreover, the language and area concept tends to focus attention on the disciplines in
the humanities and social sciences. Within these limitations one
finds relatively more information available on agriculture and the
biological sciences than on the physical sciences (with the exception of geology) and technology.

Library of Congress acquisition policy for this area calls
for the purchase of all materials which contain the results of
original research (except in the fields of agriculture and medicine), in addition to reference tools--dictionaries, bibliographies,
abstracts (120), and the like. The Library does not, however,
attempt to obtain translations of English language publications into
Portuguese. Among the 600,000 technical reports in the Science
and Technology Division there are none from Brazil. Purdue has
placed blanket orders for Brazilian publications in the fields of
its Farmington Plan assignment (physics, zoology, agriculture in
general, plant culture and horticulture in general, photography,
and home economics) (124), but has not received many publications. In 1956 the Midwest Inter-Library Center and its member
libraries began a program to acquire every serial abstracted in
Chemical Abstracts and Biological Abstracts. Although the published list of serials (57) which the Center now receives provides
no approach by country, examination does reveal a number of
Brazilian titles--e.g., Brasil Açucareiro, Brasil Médico, Brasil

Textil, the Boletim Técnico of the Instituto Agronómico do Norte
and of the Instituto Agronómico do Sul, and several university publications. Cornell reports 329 volumes classified as science and
agriculture, while Michigan has eighty-eight titles in these areas.
It should be noted that Pan American Union does not collect in the
fields of pure and applied sciences.

AGRICULTURE

        Since the National Agricultural Library attempts to collect
all significant publications, regardless of language, in its areas
of specialization, it would have material about Brazil in such fields
as general agriculture, animal science (including entomology,
veterinary science, and zoology), plant science (including economic and general botany, plant culture, field crops, and the like),
agricultural chemistry and agricultural engineering, soils, fertilizers and soil conservation, forestry and utilization of forest
production and agricultural products (including industrial uses).
Many of its holdings result from exchange arrangements with 120
Brazilian institutions.

        Because Library of Congress does not collect for research
purposes in this field, its holdings are limited, embracing such
items as reports of the state departments of agriculture and a few
titles on forestry and fisheries. However, in Class Q (Science)
there are over one hundred titles showing the geographical distribution of Brazilian flora and fauna. Oklahoma State has about
thirty-five linear feet of Brazilian federal and state documents,
which deal chiefly with agriculture, and Illinois currently receives
eleven Brazilian serials in general agriculture and seven in animal
husbandry, zootechnics, and veterinary medicine. Iowa State University of Science and Technolgoy has subscriptions to a number
of important Brazilian scientific journals, especially in the fields
of biology, agriculture, and veterinary science; holdings of most
are complete from volume one. Washington State's journal collection is less extensive and fewer sets are complete. Florida's
resources embrace about one hundred titles with emphasis on
coffee, sugar, and agricultural economics; the University's Agriculture Library maintains a special collection on coffee, which
would contain much information, although it is not limited to Brazil.
Purdue has a number of monographic works on coffee and other
crops, various series from the Serviço de Informação Agrícola,
the Instituto Oswaldo Cruz and bulletins from the states of Minas
Gerais, Paraná, and Sao Paulo. It is interesting to note that the
finest Portuguese item in the Arents Collection on tobacco at New
York Public (34) is Joaquim de Amorim Castro's Memoria sobre

as especias de tabaco que se cultivao no Brasil, and at Iowa and
Library of Congress (probably elsewhere as well) is found a complete collection of Karl F. P. von Martius' Flora Brasiliensis
(1824), while National Library of Medicine holds his Specimen
Materiae Medicae Brasiliensis.

MEDICINE AND BIOLOGICAL SCIENCES

In medicine and biological sciences, there are extensive
serial files at National Library of Medicine (41), including three
early Brazilian medical journals: Sociedade de Medicina, Rela-
torio dos Trabalhos (1831), Seminario de Saude Publica (1831), and
Revista Medica Fluminense (1835-36).   The earliest reference in
the Library to Brazil is contained in Marggraf's Tractatus topo-
graphicus et meteorologicus Brasiliae (1648).

Although Library of Congress makes no attempt to duplicate
the extensive holdings of National Library of Medicine, it has assembled nearly one hundred titles on medicine in Brazil.   There
are a few works on the history of medicine and medical education
in that country, but 75 per cent of the holdings relate to public
health.   Among the more interesting are several on sanitary affairs
in Rio de Janeiro and Santos at the turn of the century and a number on the special health problems of the Amazon Valley.

The Biomedical Library at California (Los Angeles) receives the principal Brazilian journals in the biological sciences
and medicine, and Michigan also acquires publications in these
fields.   Although the Biological Library at California (Berkeley)
does not consider Latin America as one of its areas of prime interest, it does add current serials and documents from Brazil,
especially in public health, entomology, and zoology.   Florida also
has material in the biological sciences.

PHYSICAL SCIENCES AND TECHNOLOGY

Holdings for physical sciences and technology are apparently limited, if two important institutions are typical.   Massachusetts Institute of Technology reports its collection too small to be
of use to a specialist in the field of Brazilian studies, and Georgia
Institute of Technology receives not a single Brazilian serial in
the fields in which it specializes (science, technology,and engineering).   Illinois receives, in general, fewer serials in the physical
sciences and technology than it does in the biological sciences.

Geology appears to be the only notable exception to this paucity of resources. The Geology Library at Columbia maintains a working collection for geology and maps; it includes 42 textbooks and atlases, 11 serials, 60 maps, and 44 topographical sheets. In addition, there are publications of the Instituto Nacional de Geografia. Holdings are being strengthened. Library of Congress's holdings include about three-fourths of the volumes issued in the Boletim series of the Divisão de Geologia e Mineralogia, other publications of the Divisão and about forty monographs dealing with both general and regional geology. Northwestern and Florida have a number of titles in this field, and resources at Illinois are better than for most other sciences. Twelve serials are currently received, including Boletim do Museu Nacional (Serie Geologia) and Geologia e Metalurgia. About thirty-six geological maps of Brazil, ranging from the entire country to parts of Minas Gerais, Paraná, Pernambuco, and Rio Grande do Norte are in the collections of the U.S. Geological Survey and the American Geographical Society (99).

Classified as technology at Library of Congress are approximately two hundred titles. In the Engineering and Building Group there are thirty-six works dealing with harbors and coast protective engineering, rivers, lakes, and water supply, and irrigation--of which a number are about the Northeast. A few titles on roads and pavements and on railroad engineering and operation are also present.

There is relatively little for the Mechanical Group. Nine monographic and about thirty serial publications on aviation are available (119); the latter include general periodicals, those of flying clubs, publications of the Departamento de Aeronáutica Civil and a few others. Holdings on mineral industries amount to fifty titles, plus one hundred in the Boletim series of the Divisão de Fomento de Produção Mineral. State material is of course most abundant on Minas Gerais.

MILITARY AND NAVAL SCIENCE

Although very little information is available about resources in military and naval science, it is not likely that many libraries possess significant holdings in this area. Most of the material on military science at Library of Congress falls into three groups: military education and training (15 titles), general works on the army and military organization (18 titles), and military law (14 titles). Even more concentration exists for naval science; the thirteen titles available consist of histories, reports of the Ministério da Marinha, and general works.

A limited amount of material is available on ships, ocean navigation, and the like. There are fourteen pilot guides for the Brazilian coasts and eight volumes on lighthouse service. The Map Division houses hydrographic charts of the Brazilian coast prepared by the Diretoria de Hidrografia e Navegação. Although there is no up-to-date indication of the holdings of New York Public (48, 93) as early as 1904 the collection contained some pilot guides and a few items on Brazilian naval history.

California (Berkeley) is the only library with complete sets of the Revista do Instituto de Geografia e História Militar do Brasil (P77) (1941-) and Subsídios para a História Marítima do Brasil (P94) (1938-). Apparently all volumes of Revista Marítima Brasileira (P90) (1881-) are not available in any American library; however, Florida, Library of Congress, and Stanford report both recent years and current subscriptions.

Cooperative Development of Resources

6

In recent years the cooperative development of resources of American research libraries has increased greatly. It is therefore appropriate to mention the effect of such plans on re- sources for Brazilian studies.

Under the Farmington Plan (124) about sixty American li- braries have accepted certain responsibilities for collecting. Two distinct patterns have evolved. Under one of them each li- brary accepts responsibility for acquisitions in certain subject areas--based on the Library of Congress Classification--and re- ceives publications forwarded by the dealer in each country where applicable (chiefly western Europe). The Library of Congress Classification for history and topography (Classes D, E, and F) and for language and literature (Class P) follows linguistic and/or political lines. Under this approach two libraries have responsi- bility for materials about Brazil: Texas for history and California (Los Angeles) for Portuguese language and literature, including Brazilian.

Under the other type of Farmington Plan coverage (applied chiefly to Asia, Africa, and Latin America) a library takes res- ponsibility for all publications of a country. Since 1961 Illinois has had such an assignment for Brazil, and in 1962 Joint Univer- sity Libraries undertook a secondary (i.e., duplicating) assign- ment.

Two libraries, moreover, maintain blanket orders for certain Brazilian publications: Wisconsin for items in the fields of geography, history, literature, political science, sociology, and philosophy, and Purdue for all subjects in the sciences for which it has Farmington Plan responsibility (see page 69). Wisconsin has also placed blanket orders with dealers in France, Germany,

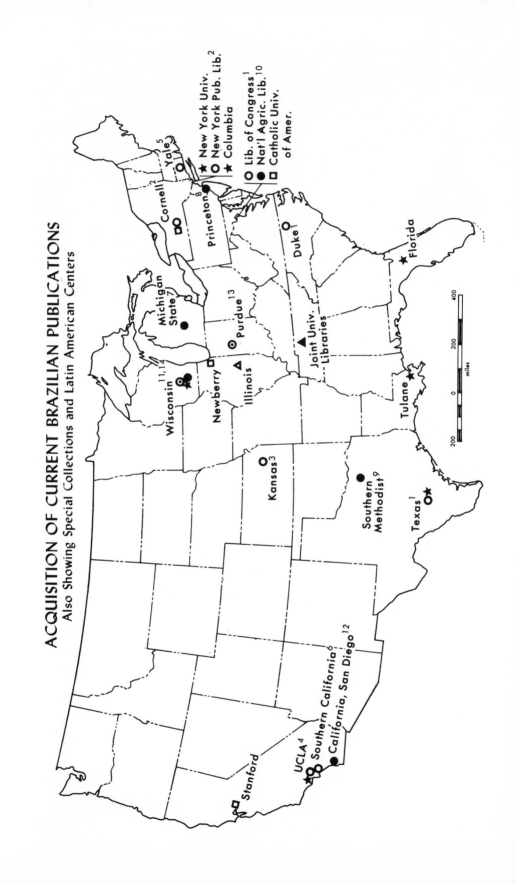

ACQUISITION OF CURRENT BRAZILIAN PUBLICATIONS
Also Showing Special Collections and Latin American Centers

Yale[5]
Cornell[2]
Princeton[8]
Duke[1]
Florida
Michigan State[7]
Purdue[13]
Joint Univ. Libraries
Wisconsin[11,14]
Newberry
Illinois
Tulane
Kansas[3]
Southern Methodist[9]
Texas[1]
Stanford
UCLA[4]
Southern California[6]
California, San Diego[12]

★ New York Univ.
O New York Pub. Lib.[2]
★ Columbia

O Lib. of Congress[1]
● Nat'l Agric. Lib.[10]
□ Catholic Univ. of Amer.

miles
200   0   200   400

LEGEND

□   Special collection of Braziliana

★   NDEA Latin American Center (Portuguese language)

◢   Farmington Plan responsibility for Brazil, except medicine (through LACAP)

◣   Blanket order as secondary Farmington Plan responsibility, except medicine, law (through LACAP)

○   LACAP blanket order with exceptions noted

    1 All except medicine

    2 All except law, agriculture, natural science, fine arts, pedagogy, religion, medicine

    3 All except law, agriculture, medicine

    4 All except engineering, technology, medicine

    5 All except law, art, sciences, agriculture, medicine

    6 All except sciences, law, agriculture, medicine

    7 All except agriculture, literature, law, religion, sciences, medicine, geography

●   LACAP blanket order for subjects noted

    8 Only literature, history, international affairs, economics, sociology, anthropology, art, architecture, political science

    9 Only economics

    10 Only agriculture and allied subjects

    11 Only land tenure, agricultural reform, economics

    12 Only medicine

◉   Other blanket order for subjects noted

    13 Only physics, zoology, agriculture, plant culture, horticulture, photography, home economics

    14 Only geography, history, literature, political science, sociology, philosophy

Italy, Mexico, Netherlands, Portugal, Spain, Sweden, and Switzerland to duplicate for its collection the items supplied to California (Los Angeles) under the latter's Farmington Plan subject assignment.

Another, and newer, program should also be described. The Latin American Cooperative Acquisitions Project (LACAP) is designed to make available all current publications of Latin American countries. Under this plan libraries place orders with Stechert-Hafner for materials from a given country or for Latin American titles in specific subject areas. Although the plan began operations in 1960, Brazilian imprints were not frequent inclusions until 1962. The following libraries are ordering Brazilian publications on a broad, although not comprehensive basis: California (Los Angeles), Cornell, Kansas, Library of Congress, Michigan State, New York Public, Princeton, Southern California, Texas, and Yale. In addition, Illinois and Joint University Libraries meet their Farmington Plan commitment by utilizing LACAP. Other libraries--California (San Diego). National Agricultural Library, Southern Methodist, and Wisconsin (Land Tenure Center)--order on a specific subject basis. The Latin American Cooperative Acquisitions Project distributed 244 Brazilian titles in 1962, 538 in 1963, and estimates the latter figure for 1964.

Finally one should mention that there are Latin American Centers for Portuguese Language at seven universities: California (Los Angeles), Columbia, Florida, New York University, Texas, Tulane, and Wisconsin. Established in recent years under the National Defense Education Act, these Centers utilize a portion of their budgets for strengthening library resources. However, no figures on the dollar amount of such support are available.

The accompanying map shows the geographical distribution of libraries involved in these projects, as well as the four which have special collections of Brazilian materials. It is interesting to note that the twenty-five institutions are located in all sections of the country, except the Pacific Northwest.

Libraries that participate in these projects are of course building their own collections, but the listing of titles so acquired in The National Union Catalog combined with inter-library loan make them available not only locally but also nationally.

 **Conclusion**

Although one of the objectives of this study is to indicate
the major American repositories of material about Brazil, the
preceding pages have dealt with resources in terms of specific
subjects. It remains to comment on the general strength of collections.

Early in this <u>Guide</u> (page 7) it was observed that of the
seventy-four institutions which furnished information for this
study twenty-three do not have significant holdings. Limited information on eight others does not permit a qualitative judgment
of their resources. It is apparent that the remaining forty-three
libraries vary in the nature and extent of their resources; a review of all available information leads one to place them in several categories on the basis of present holdings (disregarding current acquisition policies and any stated goals for the collections).

The first group consists of those institutions with outstanding resources. This means that they generally cover in considerable depth all subjects in the humanities and social sciences, all
periods of Brazilian civilization, and acquire material in a variety
of languages. Serials are not only extensive in number but embrace complete or extensive files in most cases. Holdings, ex-
ceeding 7,000 volumes or titles, would support research in most,
if not all, disciplines. Collections at seven institutions meet all
these criteria. Probably most extensive in breadth of coverage is
Library of Congress, whose classified collections contain over
12,700 titles on Brazil (in addition to resources in the Law Library and of non-book material). While strongest in literature,
history, and topography, resources are particularly significant in
all social sciences and contain representation in every subject
area. Holdings at Pan American Union include 9,000 volumes and
27,000 pieces (unbound periodicals, photographs, maps, sheet

music, and scores) with notable coverage of politics and foreign affairs, history, literature, bibliography and library science, and official publications. A statement on the general nature of the Oliveira Lima Library at Catholic University appears on page 8; it might be observed at this point that holdings are especially strong for the period through the nineteenth and early twentieth centuries and that they provide a wealth of supporting material on Brazil's Portuguese heritage.

All fields of knowledge, including law and the sciences, are very well represented in the 10,000 volumes at Texas. Additions now amount to over 1,000 volumes a year. At Berkeley, California's 9,000 volumes reflect more emphasis on the colonial period for the social sciences and on the modern period for literature, and the southern part of Brazil is best represented in all fields but literature. New York Public, with over 8,500 titles, appears to be especially strong in the social sciences. Harvard holds 7,000 volumes in the areas of history, geography, economic conditions, literature, and bound periodicals, although Argentine holdings are probably the strongest in the Latin American field.

A second category embraces libraries possessing strong but not outstanding collections. Resources are smaller in quantity, may not emphasize quite as wide a range of subject fields, and contain fewer significant journal files. Holdings in major areas at Cornell surpass 3,000 volumes with coverage chiefly of nineteenth and twentieth century publications , aside from earlier items in the Hull Collection (see page 8). Extensive holdings of nineteenth century material in Stanford's Branner collection (see page 8) provided a good foundation for the collection. Columbia reports approximately 2,700 titles dealing with Brazil, with notable strength in such professional fields as library science, architecture, and education. Florida's holdings appear to be concentrated in the social sciences; approximately two-thirds of over 2,000 titles fall in these disciplines (not counting 1,000 volumes in law). The collection at Illinois, while strong in subjects like language, literature, geography, history, and political science, is not as well developed in law, anthropology, education, philosophy, religion, and sociology; holdings in the first four disciplines come to about 3,500 volumes. At Wisconsin there are approximately 2,700 volumes (exclusive of periodicals) in literature, history, and topography, but nearly all subjects have some representation. Duke's holdings (about 5,500 volumes) are distinctive in their documentary character and in contemporary source material, while the rather extensive collection at New Mexico numbers 4,500 volumes in the two areas it has emphasized: language and literature; history and geography. The Greenlee Collection (see page 8) at Newberry, together with the Ayer Collection, provides extensive resources for nearly all phases of Brazilian civilization, but with concentration upon the colonial period.

A third group consists of those collections which might be characterized as better than average. They are, on the whole, smaller than those in the preceding class and may stress only selected areas aside from literature and history, but would contain at least 2,000 volumes or titles. Such institutions are California (Los Angeles), Indiana, Joint University Libraries, New York University, Pennsylvania, and Yale. Approaching them in size are holdings at certain universities which do not, however, consider Brazil as one of their major interests: Chicago, Michigan, North Carolina, Northwestern, and Virginia. In these cases, should institutional policy change, it would be relatively easy to develop holdings, because much basic material is already present.

Finally one notes a fourth level of resources, the working collection which is probably not extensive enough to support a great deal of research on Brazilian topics. It is found at institutions which have not, with some exceptions, emphasized Latin American studies: Brown, Iowa, Kansas, Louisiana, Minnesota, Missouri, Ohio State, Oklahoma, Princeton, Syracuse, Tulane, and Washington (Seattle).

To recapitulate, there are seven institutions with outstanding resources, nine with strong holdings, eleven with better than average, and twelve with working collections.

One should also mention those libraries which do not fit into the above scheme, because they attempt to collect only in certain limited areas: National Agricultural Library, National Library of Medicine, and Purdue. Hispanic Society has always been relatively weak in Brazilian holdings, but it has limited its efforts to the colonial period.

Another generalization concerns the geographic distribution of resources. The best collections are concentrated in two areas: Washington and New York (also the cities with greatest general strength of library resources). With the holdings available at Library of Congress, Pan American Union, and Catholic University the resources found in the nation's capital are unsurpassed. Four collections--those at New York Public, Columbia, New York University, and Hispanic Society--contribute to making the country's largest city a center of resources for Brazilian studies. The San Francisco Bay area, with two significant collections, probably ranks ahead of Chicago, because the latter lacks an outstanding collection, although it has Newberry and fairly extensive general holdings at Northwestern and Chicago. If the area is extended to include Madison and Urbana, the resources available might match those of the Bay region.

This guide also shows that strength in subject fields varies. Three--geography (including description and travel), history and literature--are most developed in each of the four types of collections. One notes, however, a growing interest in the social sciences, especially in such fields as economics and business, anthropology and sociology, political science and law.

Three factors--the increasing awareness in this country of the importance of Latin America, the concept of area study programs in universities, and the continual strengthening of research libraries--make it safe to predict that in the years ahead we shall see more and better resources for Brazilian studies in the United States.

BIBLIOGRAPHY

1. American Geographical Society of New York. Library. *Research Catalog*. Boston, G. K. Hall, 1962. 15 v.

    See vol. 7, pp. 4847-5034, for entries on Brazil.

2. Ash, Lee, comp. *Subject Collections*. 2d ed. New York, Bowker, 1961.

3. Bealer, Lewis W. "Some Recent Additions to the South American Collection in the University of California Libraries." *Hispanic American Historical Review*, XII (1932), 103-126.

4. Benson, Nettie Lee. "The Making of the Latin American Collection." *In:* Texas. University. Library. *The Library Chronicle*, VII (Summer 1962), 1-5.

5. Bibliographical Planning Committee of Philadelphia. "Philadelphia Libraries and Their Holdings." *In:* Its *Philadelphia Libraries; A Survey of Facilities, Needs and Opportunities*. Philadelphia, University of Pennsylvania Press, 1942, Supplement.

6. Boston. Public Library. *Catalogue of the Spanish Library and of the Portuguese Books Bequeathed by George Ticknor, Together with the Collection of Spanish and Portuguese Literature in the General Library*. By James Lyman Whitney. Boston, Printed by Order of the Trustees, 1879.

7. Boxer, Charles R. "The William B. Greenlee Collection." *Newberry Library Bulletin*, 2d ser., no. 6 (May 1951), 167-178.

8. Brown, Elizabeth Gasper. *Legal Education at Michigan, 1859-1959*. Ann Arbor, 1959.

9. Brown, Karl, comp. *A Guide to the Reference Collections of the New York Public Library*. New York, New York Public Library, 1941.

10. California. University. Library. *Spain and Spanish America in the Libraries of the University of California*. Berkeley, 1928-30. 2 v.

    Contains a few entries relating to Brazil.

11. California. University. University at Los Angeles. Library. *Dictionary Catalog*. Boston, G. K. Hall, 1963. 129 v.

    See vol. 14, pp. 880-990, for entries beginning "Brazil" and "Brazilian."

12. Cardozo, Manoel S. "A Guide to the Manuscripts in the Lima Library, the Catholic University of America." *In: Handbook of Latin American Studies,* no. 6. Cambridge, Harvard University Press, 1941, pp. 471-504.

13. Castañeda, Carlos E. and Dabbs, J. Autrey. "The Manuel E. Gondra Collection." *In: Handbook of Latin American Studies,* no. 6. Cambridge, Harvard University Press, 1941, pp. 505-517.

14. Catholic University of America. Library. *Bibliographical and Historical Description of the Rarest Books in the Oliveira Lima Collection.* Comp. by Ruth E. V. Holmes. Washington, 1926.

15. Chase, Gilbert. *A Guide to the Music of Latin America.* 2d ed. A Joint Publication of the Pan American Union and the Library of Congress. Washington, Pan American Union, 1962.

16. Chicago. University. Library. *Atlases in Libraries of Chicago; A Bibliography and Union Check List.* Chicago, 1936.

    Locates copies in the University of Chicago, John Crerar Library and Newberry Library.

17. Childs, James B. "The Bibliophilic Societies of South America." *Revista Interamericana de Bibliografía,* II (1952), 43-47.

18. Cobb, Gwendolin B. "Bancroft Library Microfilm: Portugal and her Empire." *Hispanic American Historical Review,* XXXIV (1954), 114-125.

19. Columbia University. Libraries. Avery Architectural Library. *Catalog of the Avery Memorial Architectural Library of Columbia University.* Comp. under the direction of James Grote van Derpool. Boston, Microphotography Co., 1958. 6 v.

20. Columbia University. Libraries. Library of the School of Library Service. *Dictionary Catalog.* Boston, G. K. Hall, 1962. 7 v.

21. Columbia University. President's Committee on the Educational Future of the University. Subcommittee on the University Libraries. *The Columbia University Libraries.* [By] Maurice F. Tauber, C. Donald Cook and Richard H. Logsdon. New York, Columbia University Press, 1958.

22. "Documentary Collections." *Hispanic American Historical Review,* XX (1940), 473-474.

    On the Oliveira Lima Library at the Catholic University of America.

23. Downs, Robert B. "Leading American Library Collections." *Library Quarterly,* XII (1942), 457-473.

24. Downs, Robert B. "Notable Materials Added to American Libraries, 1938-39." *Library Quarterly,* X (1940), 157-191.

_____. _____, 1939-40. *Ibid.,* XI (1941), 257-301.

_____. _____, 1940-41. *Ibid.,* XII (1942), 175-220.

Van Male, John. _____, 1941-42. *Ibid.,* XIV (1944), 132-158.

Hintz, Carl W. _____, 1943-47. *Ibid.,* XIX (1949), 105-118, 186-200.

_____. _____, 1948-49. *Ibid.,* XXI (1951), 183-197, 267-284.

25. Downs, Robert B. *Resources of New York City Libraries.* Chicago, American Library Association, 1942.

26. Fein, John M. "Resources in the Field of Latin American Studies in Libraries of the Southeast." *Southeastern Librarian,* V (1955), 91-98.

27. Gardel, Luis D. *A Brief Description of Some Rare and Interesting Books From the XVIth and XVIIth Centuries, Which Can Be Found in the Columbus Memorial Library.* Washington, Pan American Union, 1958.

    In the Columbus Memorial Library, Pan American Union.

28. Gorham, Rex. "The Folkways of Brazil." *Bulletin of the New York Public Library,* XLVII (1943), 255-272, 427-435; XLVIII (1944), 435-440, 501-511.

    Reprinted (See below).

29. _____. *The Folkways of Brazil; A Bibliography.* New York, New York Public Library, 1944.

    A corrected and enlarged reprint of the above. Based on holdings of the New York Public Library; locates books not in that Library (chiefly in Library of Congress).

30. Harrison, John P. "The Archives of United States Diplomatic and Consular Posts in Latin America." *Hispanic American Historical Review,* XXXIII (1953), 168-183.

31. _____. *Guide to Materials on Latin America in the National Archives.* (National Archives Publication, no. 62-3) Washington,

General Services Administration, National Archives and Records Service, National Archives, 1961-

To be complete in 2 vols.

32. Hasse, A. R. "Check List of Foreign Government Documents on Finance in the New York Public Library." *Bulletin of the New York Public Library,* V (1901), 457-486.

See pp. 459-460 for items on Brazil.

33. _____. "List of Books and Some Articles in Periodicals in the New York Public Library, Relating to Political Rights, Constitutions and Constitutional Law." *Bulletin of the New York Public Library,* VIII (1904), 22-36, 52-88, 103-138, 155-198.

See pp. 59-60 for items on Brazil.

34. Hilton, Ronald, ed. *Handbook of Hispanic Source Materials and Research Organizations in the United States.* 2d ed. Stanford, Stanford University Press, 1956.

The index has 71 references to Brazil, but not all deal with library resources.

35. "Hispanic American Government Documents in the Library of Congress." *Hispanic American Historical Review,* VI (1926), 134-141.

36. Hispanic Society of America. Library. *Catalogue.* Boston, G. K. Hall, 1962. 10 v.

See vol. 3, pp. 1460-1494, for entries beginning "Brazil" and "Brazilian."

37. _____. *List of Books Printed before 1601 in the Library of the Hispanic Society of America.* By Clara Louisa Penney. Offset reissue, with additions. New York, Printed by Order of the Trustees, Hispanic Society of America, 1955.

38. _____. *List of Books Printed 1601-1700, in the Library of the Hispanic Society of America.* By Clara Louisa Penney. New York, Printed by Order of the Trustees, 1938.

39. Hoole, William Stanley, ed. *Foreign Newspapers in Southeastern Libraries.* Sponsored by the Association of Southeastern Research Libraries. University, Alabama, University of Alabama, 1963.

40. Hussey, Roland Dennis. "Manuscript Hispanic Americana in the Harvard College Library." *Hispanic American Historical Review*, XVII (1937), 259-277.

    Contains a few entries relating to Brazil.

41. Jones, Harold W. "Central and South American Literature in the Army Medical Library [i.e., National Library of Medicine]." *In:* Inter-American Bibliographical and Library Association. *Proceedings*, 3d. New York, Wilson, 1941, pp. 66-82.

42. Kruzas, Anthony T., ed. *Directory of Special Libraries and Information Centers.* 1st ed. Detroit, Gale Research Co. [1963]

43. Law Librarians' Society of Washington, D. C. *Union List of Legal Periodicals, District of Columbia Area.* Comp. by Committee on Legal Periodicals of the Law Librarians' Society of Washington, D. C., Chapter of the American Association of Law Libraries. Fairfax, Va., Coiner Publications [1963]

44. *List of Serial Publications of Foreign Governments, 1815-1931.* Ed. by Winifred Gregory. New York, Wilson, 1932.

    Lists holdings of various libraries.

45. "List of Works in the New York Public Library Relating to Criminology." *Bulletin of the New York Public Library*, XV (1911), 259-317, 350-371, 379-446, 463-501, 515-557, 567-621, 635-714.

    See pp. 464-465 for items on Brazil.

46. "List of Works in the New York Public Library Relating to Hydraulic Engineering." *Bulletin of the New York Public Library*, XI (1907), 512-552, 565-626.

    See pp. 568 and 602 for items on Brazil.

47. "List of Works in the New York Public Library Relating to Money and Banking." *Bulletin of the New York Public Library*, XII (1908), 192-228, 239-282, 295-331, 346-399.

    See pp. 219 and 242 for items on Brazil.

48. "List of Works in the New York Public Library Relating to Nautical and Naval Art and Science, Navigation and Seamanship,

Shipbuilding, etc." *Bulletin of the New York Public Library,*
XI (1907), 239-287, 299-345, 359-398, 420-436.

See p. 277 for items on Brazil.

49. "List of Works in the New York Public Library Relating to
Numismatics." *Bulletin of the New York Public Library,*
XVII (1913), 981-1049; XVIII (1914), 59-86, 149-175, 404-428.

See vol. 17, pp. 1024-1025, for items on Brazil.

50. Luper, Albert Thomas. *The Music of Brazil.* ([Pan American Union. Division of Music and Visual Arts] Music Series,
no. 9) Washington, Pan American Union, 1943.

Nearly all items in Pan American Union.

51. Manchester, Alan K. "Descriptive Bibliography of the Brazilian Section of the Duke University Library." *Hispanic American Historical Review,* XIII (1933), 238-266, 495-523.

Reprinted. [Durham, N.C., 1933]

52. _____. "Recent Additions to the Brazilian Collection in the
Duke University Library." *Hispanic American Historical
Review,* XI (1931), 135-136.

53. "Manuscript Collections in the New York Public Library."
Bulletin of the New York Public Library, V (1901), 306-336.

See p. 318 for manuscripts pertaining to Brazil.

54. Marchant, Alexander D. "The Oliveira Lima Collection."
Bulletin of the Pan American Union, LXVII (1933), 721-728.

In Catholic University of America Library.

55. Martin, Lawrence. "South American Cartographic Treasures."
*Library of Congress Quarterly Journal of Current Acquisi-
tions,* I (Jan./Mar. 1944), 30-39.

56. "Materials Relating to Brazil in the National Archives." *Hispanic American Historical Review,* XXII (1942), 521-528.

57. Midwest Inter-Library Center. *Rarely Held Scientific Serials
in the Midwest Inter-Library Center.* Chicago, 1963.

_____. _____. *Supplement.* Chicago, 1964.

58. Moraes, Rubens Borba de. *Bibliographia Brasiliana: A Bibliographical Essay on Rare Books About Brazil Published
from 1504 to 1900 and Works of Brazilian Authors Published*

Abroad before the Independence of Brazil in 1822. Amsterdam, Rio de Janeiro, Colibris, Editora, 1958. 2 v.

> *Locates copies of some items in Brown University, Harvard University, Henry E. Huntington Library, Library of Congress, New York Public Library and elsewhere.*

59. Moser, Gerald M. "Portuguese Pamphlets." *Newberry Library Bulletin,* III No. 7 (November 1954), 206-215.

    > *Some pamphlets deal with Brazil.*

60. *The National Union Catalog; A Cumulative Author List Representing Library of Congress Printed Cards and Titles Reported by Other American Libraries.* Jan. 1956-*to date.* Washington, Library of Congress, 1956-*to date.*

    > *Printed in 9 monthly issues, 3 quarterly cumulations, annual cumulations for four years and a quinquennial in the fifth.*

61. *The National Union Catalog, 1952-1955 Imprints; An Author List Representing Library of Congress Printed Cards and Titles Reported by Other American Libraries.* Ann Arbor, Edwards, 1961. 30 v.

62. *The National Union Catalog of Manuscript Collections, 1959-1961; Based on Reports from American Repositories of Manuscripts.* Ann Arbor, Edwards, 1962.

    _____, *1962.* Hamden, Conn., Shoe String Press, 1964.

    _____. *Index, 1959-1962.* Hamden, Conn., Shoe String Press, 1964.

63. *New Serial Titles, 1950-1960. Supplement to the Union List of Serials Third Edition. A Union List of Serials Commencing Publication After December 31, 1949.* Prepared under the Sponsorship of the Joint Committee on the Union List of Serials. Washington, Library of Congress, 1961. 2 v.

    > *Continued by monthly issues with annual cumulations, which are self-cumulative through periods of at least five years.*

64. New York. Metropolitan Museum of Art. *Books on Latin America and its Art in the Metropolitan Museum of Art Library.* Comp. by John B. Montignani. [New York] 1943.

65. New York. Metropolitan Museum of Art. Library. *Library Catalog.* Boston, G. K. Hall, 1960. 25 v.

_____. _____. *Supplement.* 1st. Boston, G. K. Hall, 1962.

66. New York. Public Library. Reference Department. *Dictionary Catalog of the History of the Americas.* Boston, G. K. Hall, 1961. 28 v.

   See vol. 3, pp. 2659-2823, for entries beginning "Brazil".

67. Newberry Library. *A Catalog of the William B. Greenlee Collection of Portuguese History and Literature and the Portuguese Materials in the Newberry Library.* Comp. by Doris Varner Welsh. Chicago, 1953.

   See pp. 140-195 for holdings on Brazil. A new edition is in preparation.

68. _____. Edward E. Ayer Collection. *Dictionary Catalog of the Edward E. Ayer Collection of Americana and American Indians.* Boston, G. K. Hall, 1961. 16 v.

   See vol. 2, pp. 912-963, for entries beginning "Brazil" and "Brazilian."

69. Norman, James. "Researcher's Paradise." *Americas,* XV (Jan. 1963), 19-21.

   On Latin American Collection at University of Texas.

70. Northwestern University. School of Law. Library. *Guide to the Legal Collections in Chicago.* Comp. by Kurt Schwerin. Chicago, Pub. for the Chicago Association of Law Libraries by Northwestern University Law Library, c1955.

71. Oliveira Lima, Manoel de. "The Portuguese Manuscripts in the Ibero-American Library at the Catholic University of America." *Hispanic American Historical Review,* VIII (1928), 261-280.

   Part III covers India and Brazil.

72. Pan American Union. Columbus Memorial Library. *Bibliografía de la Literatura sobre Educación de Adultos en América Latina.* (Bibliographic Series, no. 37) Washington, 1952.

   See pp. 11-17 for items on Brazil. Based chiefly on holdings of Library of Congress and Pan American Union.

73. Pan American Union. Columbus Memorial Library. *Bibliography on Public Administration in Latin America.* Comp. by Jorge Grossman. 2d ed. (Bibliographic Series, no. 43) Washington, 1958.

  > *Each division contains section on Brazil. Based on holdings of Institute of Inter-American Affairs, Library of Congress and Pan American Union.*

74. _____. _____. *La Biblioteca Pública en América: Una Bibliografía Selecta.* Comp. by Marietta Daniels. (Bibliographic Series, no. 34) Washington, 1951.

  > *Includes items on Brazil. Based on holdings of Library of Congress and Pan American Union.*

75. _____. _____. *Books and Magazine Articles on Geography in the Columbus Memorial Library of the Pan American Union.* (Bibliographic Series, no. 13) Washington [1935?]

  > *See pp. 8-13 for items on Brazil.*

76. _____. _____. *Catalogue of Newspapers and Magazines in the Columbus Memorial Library of the Pan American Union.* (Bibliographic Series, no. 6) Washington, 1931.

  > *See pp. 13-20 for Brazilian titles.*

77. _____. _____. *Current Latin American Periodicals Relating to Economic Subjects in the Library of the Pan American Union.* (Bibliographic Series, no. 20) Washington, 1938.

  > *See pp. 7-14 for Brazilian titles.*

78. _____. _____. *List of Books Accessioned and Periodical Articles Indexed in the Columbus Memorial Library.* August 1950- *to date.* Washington, 1950- *to date.*

79. _____. _____. *A List of Literary and Cultural Magazines Received in the Columbus Memorial Library of the Pan American Union.* (Bibliographic Series, no. 22) Washington, 1940.

  > *See pp. 5-7 for Brazilian titles.*

80. _____. _____. *Maps Relating to Latin America in Books and Periodicals.* Comp. by A. Curtis Wilgus. (Bibliographic Series, no. 10) Washington, 1933.

  > *Most divisions contain sections on Brazil. Based on holdings of Library of Congress and Pan American Union.*

81. Pan American Union. Columbus Memorial Library. *Recent Trends in Inter-American Relations, A Bibliography.* (Bibliographic Series, no. 21) Washington, 1939.

> *See pp. 27 and 47 for items relating to Brazil. In Pan American Union.*

82. _____. _____. *A Selected List of Latin American Periodicals Containing Laws and Legal Information.* (Bibliographic Series, no. 28) Washington, 1942.

> *See pp. 8-10 for items on Brazil. Based on holdings of Library of Congress and Pan American Union.*

83. _____. _____. *Union List of Latin American Newspapers in Libraries in the United States.* Comp. by Arthur E. Gropp. (Bibliographic Series, no. 39) Washington, 1958.

> *See pp. 39-52 for Brazilian titles.*

84. Pound, Roscoe. "The Harvard Law Library." *Harvard Library Bulletin,* V (1951), 290-303.

85. Ramalho, Américo da Costa. " 'The Portuguese Pamphlets.' " *Library of Congress Quarterly Journal of Current Acquisitions,* XX (1962-63), 157-162.

> *Some items deal with Brazil. In Library of Congress.*

86. "Reference Department Acquisitions during 1961-62, Part II." *Bulletin of the New York Public Library,* LXVII (1963), 237-251.

87. Reichman, Felix. *Sugar, Gold, and Coffee; Essays on the History of Brazil Based on Francis Hull's Books.* Ithaca, Cornell University Library, 1959.

88. Robertson, James Alexander. "The Oliveira Lima Collection of Hispanoamericana." *Hispanic American Historical Review,* III (1920), 78-83.

> *In Catholic University of America Library.*

89. Rogers, Francis Millet. "William Brooks Greenlee, Scholar and Benefactor of Portuguese Studies." *Hispanic American Historical Review,* XXXIII (1953), 587-589.

90. Sabin, Joseph. *Bibliotheca Americana. A Dictionary of Books Relating to America, from its Discovery to the Present Time.* Begun by Joseph Sabin, continued by Wilberforce Eames and

completed by R. W. G. Vail for the Bibliographical Society of America. New York, J. Sabin [etc.] 1868-1936. 29 v.

Locates copies in many libraries. See vol. 2, pp. 429-448, for special section under "Brazil."

91. Schwerin, Kurt. "Foreign Legal Periodicals in American Law Libraries — A Union List." *Law Library Journal*, LIV (1961), 145-164.

92. _____. "Law Libraries and Foreign Law Collections in the U. S. A." *International and Comparative Law Quarterly*, XI (1962), 537-562.

93. "A Selected List of Works in the New York Public Library Relating to Naval History, Naval Administration, etc." *Bulletin of the New York Public Library*, VIII (1904), 261-295, 323-351, 369-393, 423-463, 560-575.

See p. 265 for items on Brazilian Navy.

94. Smith, Robert C. *Franz Frühbeck's Brazilian Journey; A Study of Some Paintings and Drawings Made in the Years 1817 and 1818 and Now in the Possession of the Hispanic Society of America.* Philadelphia, University of Pennsylvania Press [and] Hispanic Society of America [1960]

95. _____. "Requena and the Japurá: Some Eighteenth Century Watercolors of the Amazon and Other Rivers." *The Americas*, III (1946-47), 31-65.

In Oliveira Lima Library, Catholic University of America. Also mentions 8 Requena maps in Map Division, Library of Congress.

96. "Source Material in Education from Latin America." *In:* Teachers College Library. *Book News and Notes,* no. 29 (April 17, 1963).

97. Spell, Lota M. *Research Materials for the Study of Latin America at the University of Texas.* (Texas. University. Institute of Latin American Studies. Latin American Studies, 14) Austin, University of Texas Press, 1954.

98. Stetson, John B., Jr. "A Letter of Appraisal." *Harvard Library Notes,* no. 4 (April 1921), 83-84.

On Harvard's resources.

99. Sullivan, Henry B. *A Catalogue of Geological Maps of South America.* (American Geographical Society. Research Series, no. 9) New York, American Geographical Society, 1922.

100. Taylor, Marion. *Guide to Latin American Reference Material; A Union List for Use in the Atlanta-Athens Area.* (SLA Regional Bibliographies, no. 1). Atlanta, Special Libraries Association, Georgia Chapter, 1958.

    Locates copies in 14 libraries in the Atlanta-Athens area.

101. Texas. University. Library. *Calendar of the Manuel E. Gondra Manuscript Collection of the University of Texas Library.* Prepared by Carlos Eduardo Castañeda and Jack Autrey Dabbs. Mexico, Editorial Jus, 1952.

102. _____. *Recent Brazilian Acquisitions, Latin American Collection.* [Austin, 1963]

103. Thompson, Lawrence S. "Resources for Research in Latin American Literature in Southern Libraries." *In:* South Atlantic Modern Language Association. *South Atlantic Studies for Sturgis E. Leavitt.* Ed. by Thomas B. Stroup and Sterling A. Stoudemire. Washington, Scarecrow Press, 1953, pp. 97-108.

104. *Union List of Serials in Libraries of the United States and Canada.* 2d ed. Ed. by Winifred Gregory. New York, Wilson, 1943.

    _____. _____. *Supplement, Jan. 1941-Dec. 1943.* New York, Wilson, 1945.

    _____. _____. *Supplement, Jan. 1944-Dec. 1949.* New York, Wilson, 1953.

    The third edition is in preparation.

105. U. S. Library of Congress. *Annual Report of the Librarian of Congress.* Washington, U. S. Govt. Print. Off.

    a. *1913,* pp. 31-34.

    b. *1915,* pp. 53-55.

    c. *1928,* p. 35.

    d. *1930,* pp. 54-55.

    e. *1940,* pp. 71-72.

    f. *1941,* p. 95.

    g. *1943,* pp. 155-156.

106. U. S. Library of Congress. *A Guide to the Official Publications of the Other American Republics. III. Brazil.* Comp. by John de Noia. (Latin American Series, no. 35) Washington, 1948.

> *Official publications — serials, series and monographs — as recorded in the Library's catalogs.*

107. ____. *Information Bulletin.* v. 1-21; Jan. 23, 1942-Dec. 31, 1962. Washington, 1942-62.

108. ____. *Library of Congress Catalog — Books: Subjects; A Cumulative List of Works Represented by Library of Congress Printed Cards.* Ann Arbor, Mich., Edwards; Paterson, N. J., Pageant Books; Washington, Library of Congress, 1955-63. 51 v.

> *See 1950-54 cumulation, vol. 3, pp. 56-77; 1955-59 cumulation, vol. 3, pp. 285-310; 1960 cumulation, vol. 1, pp. 355-360; 1961 cumulation, vol. 1, pp. 367-371; 1962 cumulation, vol. 1, pp. 382-389, for entries beginning "Brazil" and "Brazilian."*

109. ____. *A List of Books, Magazine Articles and Maps Relating to Brazil, 1800-1900.* Comp. by Philip Lee Phillips. Washington, U. S. Govt. Print. Off., 1901.

> *Locates copies in Coast and Geodetic Survey, Department of State and Library of Congress.*

110. ____. *Newspapers on Microfilm.* 5th ed. Comp. under the direction of George A. Schwegmann, Jr. Washington, 1963.

> *See p. 233 for Brazilian titles.*

111. ____. "Portuguese Collection." [Washington, 1929?]

> *Typewritten list of collection acquired in 1928. Some items deal with Brazil.*

112. ____. *Quarterly Journal of Current Acquisitions.* v. 1-20; July/Sept. 1943-Aug. 1963. [Washington, 1943-63]

> a. vol. 5, p. 26 (Nov. 1947)
>
> b. vol. 5, p. 30 (Nov. 1947)
>
> c. vol. 14, p. 53 (Nov. 1956)
>
> d. vol. 17, p. 62 (Nov. 1959)

113. U. S. Library of Congress. Census Library Project. *General Censuses and Vital Statistics in the Americas.* Washington, U. S. Govt. Print. Off., 1943.

> *See pp. 13-22 for Brazil. Based on holdings of Library of Congress; locates copies not in its collections.*

114. _____. Law Library. *Guide to the Law and Legal Literature of Argentina, Brazil and Chile.* By E. M. Borchard. Washington, U. S. Govt. Print. Off., 1917.

> *See pp. 191-364 for Brazil. Based on holdings of Library of Congress. A supplement covering the period since 1917 is in preparation.*

115. _____. _____. *Legal Codes of the Latin American Republics.* (Latin American Series, no. 1) Washington, 1942.

> *For description of Brazilian Codes see pp. 9-11 (in English), 50-51 (in Spanish) and 76-77 (in Portuguese). Based on holdings of Library of Congress.*

116. _____. Map Division. *Check List of Large Scale Maps Published by Foreign Governments (Great Britain Excepted) in the Library of Congress.* Comp. under the direction of Philip Lee Phillips. Washington, U. S. Govt. Print. Off., 1904.

117. _____. _____. *A List of Geographical Atlases in the Library of Congress, with Bibliographical Notes.* Washington, U. S. Govt. Print. Off., 1909-63. 6 v.

118. _____. Reference Dept. *Guide to the Special Collections of Prints and Photographs in the Library of Congress.* Comp. by Paul Vanderbilt. Washington, 1955.

119. _____. Science and Technology Division. *Aeronautical and Space Serial Publications; A World List.* Washington, 1962.

> *Gives call numbers of items in Library of Congress.*

120. _____. _____. *A Guide to the World's Abstracting and Indexing Services in Science and Technology.* [Prepared for the National Federation of Science Abstracting and Indexing Services] (National Federation of Science Abstracting and Indexing Services. Report, no. 102) Washington, 1963.

> *Gives call numbers of items in Library of Congress, National Agricultural Library and National Library of Medicine.*

121. U. S. National Archives. *List of Foreign Service Post Records in the National Archives.* Comp. by Mark G. Eckhoff and Alexander P. Mavro (Special Lists, no. 9). Washington, The National Archives, National Archives and Records Service, General Services Administration, 1952.

122. _____. *Materials in the National Archives Relating to Brazil.* (Reference Information Circular, no. 8) Washington [1942]

123. _____. *Materials Relating to Latin America in Records of Emergency War Agencies, 1917-19, in the National Archives.* (Reference Information Circular, no. 11) [Washington] 1942.

124. Williams, Edwin E. *Farmington Plan Handbook.* Rev. to 1961 and Abridged. [Ithaca, N. Y.] Association of Research Libraries, 1961.

125. Wisconsin. University. Land Tenure Center. Library. *Bibliography: Agrarian Reform and Tenure. With Special Sections on Agricultural Finance, Taxation and Agriculture, Agricultural Statistics and Bibliographical Sources.* Madison, 1964.

APPENDICES

 LIBRARIES

WHICH SUPPLIED INFORMATION

American Antiquarian Society
Boston Public Library
Boston University
Brown University
University of California (Berkeley)
University of California (Los Angeles)
Catholic University of America
University of Chicago
University of Cincinnati
Cleveland Public Library
Columbia University
University of Connecticut
Cornell University
Duke University
Emory University
University of Florida
Florida State University
Georgia Institute of Technology
Harvard University
Hispanic Society of America
University of Illinois
Indiana University
State University of Iowa
Iowa State University of Science and Technology
Johns Hopkins University
Joint University Libraries
University of Kansas
University of Kentucky
Library of Congress
Louisiana State University
University of Maryland

Massachusetts Institute of Technology
University of Miami
University of Michigan
Midwest Inter-Library Center
University of Minnesota
University of Missouri
National Agricultural Library
National Library of Medicine
University of Nebraska
University of New Mexico
New York Public Library
New York State Library
New York University
Newberry Library
University of North Carolina
Northwestern University
University of Notre Dame
Ohio State University
University of Oklahoma
Oklahoma State University
University of Oregon
Pan American Union
University of Pennsylvania
Pennsylvania State University
University of Pittsburgh
Princeton University
Purdue University
University of Rochester
Saint Louis University
University of Southern California
Stanford University
Syracuse University
University of Tennessee
University of Texas
Tulane University
University of Utah
University of Virginia
University of Washington (Seattle)
Washington State University
Washington University (St. Louis)
Wayne State University
University of Wisconsin
Yale University

BRAZILIAN
2 ◆ PERIODICALS
IN THE HUMANITIES & SOCIAL SCIENCES

INTRODUCTORY NOTE

Some years ago, at the first International Colloquium on
Luso-Brazilian Studies, L. L. Barrett of Washington and Lee
University suggested "the compilation of a descriptive index of
all serial publications in this country and abroad that contain
materials essential to the complete study of any phase of Brazilian literature" with indication of the library or libraries where
they are available.* The present union list is both more and
less than what he called for. It is, in the first place, selective
rather than comprehensive and limited to Brazilian titles, but,
on the other hand, it is not confined to literary journals, embracing titles from the humanities and social sciences. It contains only the ninety-eight periodicals which appear in the
Zimmerman compilation.** While many titles could doubtless-
ly have been added, the task of selection would have been difficult, and a longer list would have greatly increased the burden
of checking for libraries.

Although the present effort duplicates what will be available in the third edition of the Union List of Serials (for titles
beginning publication before 1950) and what already appears in
New Serial Titles (for those beginning after that date), it provides all information in one place and reflects, in the case of

---

* L. L. Barrett, "A Proposed Descriptive Index of Periodicals Containing
   Materials Pertinent to the Study of Brazilian Literature, with a List of the
   Libraries Where These Periodicals Are Available," In International Col-
   loquium on Luso-Brazilian Studies, Proceedings (Nashville, Vanderbilt
   University Press, 1953), pp. 215-217.
** Irene Zimmerman, A Guide to Current Latin American Periodicals: Humani-
   ties and Social Sciences (Gainesville, Fla., Kallman Publishing Co., 1961).

some libraries, acquisitions made after the closing date of the
Union List of Serials.   The present list also brings to fruition
one of the resolutions of the Eighth Seminar on the Acquisition
of Latin American Library Materials.

Journals appear here in the same sequence (alphabetically
by title) as in the Zimmerman work, although they have been
numbered from one to ninety-eight to facilitate quick reference;
each entry provides title, place of publication, year begun and
frequency (a few changes in title, etc., are noted, but there was
no systematic attempt to revise bibliographic information); to
this has been added an extract from the Zimmerman annotation
to indicate scope and type of articles contained.

This union list follows the basic style of the Union List of
Serials; it uses the same symbols to represent libraries and to
show holdings, with a single addition.   Many libraries found it
impossible to supply a full statement of holdings and indicated
only that titles were present in their collections; in such instances
the symbol # follows the library's name.   As in the case of the
Union List of Serials reports of holdings arrived in varied form
--volumes, years, and whole numbers--from which the compiler
derived as much uniformity as possible.   Nevertheless, it is
probable that errors and inconsistencies remain.   The user
should also bear in mind that some libraries cautiously reported
holdings only to the date of checking (1963, or in some cases
1964); consequently, given the usual lag in journal publication,
their holdings appear to end in 1961 or 1962, although in reality
they maintain a current file and hence might well have used the
+ symbol.   Sixty-three libraries supplied partial or complete
information on their holdings.

ABBREVIATIONS AND SYMBOLS

a.	annual
bi.-m.	bimonthly
ir.	irregular
m.	monthly
no.	number(s)
n.s.	new series
q.	quarterly
s.a.	semiannual
w.	weekly
+	currently received
[ ]	incomplete
#	present in library's collection; holdings not supplied

SAMPLE STATEMENTS OF HOLDINGS

1+	complete file beginning with volume 1 and also current subscription
1-4, 8+	complete file and also current subscription, but lacking volumes 5 through 7
[1-4]+	complete file and also current subscription, but volumes 1 through 4 are incomplete
[2+]	complete file beginning with volume 2 and also current subscription, but with gaps
4-[7]	volumes 4 through 7, of which 7 is incomplete
1-[5-6]7	volumes 1 through 7, of which 5 and 6 are incomplete
1-[7[-[12]	volumes 1 through 12, of which 7 and 12 are incomplete
1,3, 5-7	incomplete file, consisting only of volumes 1,3 and 5 through 7
current issues	current issues only; no permanent file maintained

SYMBOLS FOR LIBRARIES

CLU	University of California (Los Angeles)
CSt	Stanford University
CU	University of California (Berkeley)
CtY	Yale University
DCU	Catholic University of America
DLC	Library of Congress
DNLM	National Library of Medicine
DPU	Pan American Union
FMU	University of Miami Library
FTaSU	Florida State University
FU	University of Florida
GAT	Georgia Institute of Technology
GEU	Emory University
ICMILC	Midwest Inter-Library Center
ICN	Newberry Library
ICU	University of Chicago
IEN	Northwestern University
IU	University of Illinois

IaAS	Iowa State University of Science and Technology
IaU	State University of Iowa
InNd	University of Notre Dame
InU	Indiana University
KU	University of Kansas
KyU	University of Kentucky
LNT	Tulane University
LU	Louisiana State University
MB	Boston Public Library
MCM	Massachusetts Institute of Technology
MH	Harvard University
MdBJ	Johns Hopkins University
MdU	University of Maryland
MiDW	Wayne State University
MiU	University of Michigan
MnU	University of Minnesota
MoSU	St. Louis University
MoSW	Washington University (St. Louis)
MoU	University of Missouri
N	New York State Library
NIC	Cornell University
NN	New York Public Library
NNC	Columbia University
NNH	Hispanic Society of America
NSyU	Syracuse University
NbU	University of Nebraska
NcD	Duke University
NcU	University of North Carolina
NjP	Princeton University
NmU	University of New Mexico
OCl	Cleveland Public Library
OU	Ohio State University
OkU	University of Oklahoma
OrU	University of Oregon
PPiU	University of Pittsburgh
PSt	Pennsylvania State University
PU	University of Pennsylvania
RPB	Brown University
TNJ	Joint University Libraries (Vanderbilt University, George Peabody College for Teachers, and Scarritt College)
TU	University of Tennessee
TxU	University of Texas
UU	University of Utah
ViU	University of Virginia
WU	University of Wisconsin
WaU	University of Washington

America Latina   SEE
Boletim do Centro Latino-Americano de Pesquisas em
Ciencias Sociais

1.   Anais da Associação dos Geógrafos Brasileiros.   Sao
Paulo, 1949-   a.

"Usual contents are studies recommended for inclusion by
members and accepted by the Association, but issues may
be devoted to papers delivered at a national or international
meeting.   Physical geography has predominated, but other
phases are increasingly considered.   Documentation and
supporting bibliographies vary."

CLU	1,3-7	LU	1,3-6
CSt	1-7	MH	[1-7]
CU	1,3+	N	[3-4]
DLC	1-7,10	NIC	1,3-7
DPU	1+	NN	1,5
FMU	1+	NNC	#
FU	1-2 [3-7],[11]	NSyU	#
ICU	#	NcU	#
KyU	#	TxU	1,3-7

2.   Anais da Universidade do Brasil.   Rio de Janeiro, 1950-
ir. (2 to 3 years)

"Issues vary as to the fields represented, but a preponder-
ance of articles are in scientific fields--chiefly medicine
and engineering--and law.   There are occasional articles or
lectures dealing with the fine arts, literature, philosophy,
or economics.   Relevant legislation is included."

CLU	#	KU	1-4
CSt	1-2	KyU	#
CU	1	NN	2-4
DLC	1-4	NNC	#
DPU	1+	NcU	#
GEU	[1]	TNJ	1
ICU	#	TxU	[1]
IU	1-3	ViU	1
InU	2-5		

3. Anais do Museu Histórico Nacional. Rio de Janeiro,
    1940-   s. (ir.)

    "Issues examined contain valuable studies of early Brazil-
    ian cultural history by the director of the Museum, Gustavo
    Barroso, and others, chiefly curators of the various
    sections."

CLU	#	NN	1+
CU	1+	NcU	#
CtY	3	NjP	3
DLC	1-3,5,8	TNJ	1-4
DPU	1942-43	WU	1-4
FU	8-9	WaU	7
ICU	#		

4. Anhembi. Sao Paulo, 1950-   m. Ceased publication in
    1962 with vol.48 (no.144)

    "The several articles contained cover a wide range both
    geographically and as to subject matter. One or more
    usually bear directly on Brazilian history, culture, or
    current problems, but many of the others are either of
    general interest or deal with some specific phase of a
    foreign culture."

CLU	no.105-128, 130-132,136- 138,141-144.	NN	no.29,38+
		NNC	#
CSt	10-[16],26+	NjP	no.2-29,31, 33-47,49-99
CU	1-28,31+	NmU	no.115-116, 118-120
DCU	#		
DLC	11,13-41	TNJ	1+
DPU	1+	TxU	no.78,83, 85-86,101- 102,105-144
FU	1+		
ICU	#		
IU	no.2-144	WU	no. 1-144
MH	[2-139]		

5. Anuário de imprensa, rádio, e televisão. Rio de Janeiro,
    1940-   a.

    "An editors' and publishers' yearbook, containing articles
    and data of general interest in addition to specific data con-
    cerning newspapers, arranged geographically, and a sub-
    ject listing of periodicals under some 50 headings. Data
    for periodicals include date of founding, periodicity, ad-
    dress, prices, officials, and specifications."

CU	1961/62+
DPU	1956/57
NN	1958, 1959
TxU	1961/62

6. Arquivos brasileiros de psicotécnica. Rio de Janeiro,
    1949-   q.   Fundação Getúlio Vargas. Instituto de
    Seleção e Orientação Profissional.

    "Important review in field of applied psychology. Included
    here because articles bearing on problems of education,
    sociology, or public administration are occasionally cited
    in the literature of those fields. Contains five or more
    original studies, thoroughly documented both bibliographi-
    cally and statistically, a notes and comments section, and
    a bibliographical one."

DNLM	#	MoSW	1-10
DPU	1+	NN	1+
FU	14+	NNC	#
IU	[13]	WaU	1-[7-8]-[11-12]
MH	1-13		

7. Bibliografia brasileira de educação. Rio de Janeiro, 1954- q.
    Ministério de Educação e Cultura. Instituto Nacional de
    Estudos Pedagógicos. Centro Brasileiro de Pesquisas
    Educacionais.

    "This useful bibliography lists and abstracts Brazilian
    writings concerning education, rather broadly interpreted,
    as they appear in periodicals, newspapers, books, pamph-
    lets, and processed materials such as reports of con-
    gresses."

CLU	6-9	KyU	#
CSt	[1-2] 3+	NcU	#
DLC	1+	OkU	5-9
DPU	1+	TxU	2+
FU	[2],5+	WU	[2+]
IU	[2-3]-[9]		

8. <u>Boletim bibliográfico.</u> Biblioteca Nacional. Rio de Janeiro, 1951-   s.a.

"The first of the two <u>tomos</u> registers, with full bibliographic data including prices for trade publications, the Library's receipts of Brazilian monographic publications--books, pamphlets, <u>separatas</u> from books or serials, non-serial documents, music, cinema scripts, TV programs, and maps--received on legal deposit during the first semester. The second lists in addition the titles of serials of which issues have been received during the year."

CLU	1-10	MnU	1951+
CSt	1+	NN	1951-60
CU	1+	NNC	#
CtY	1+	NSyU	#
DLC	1951-61	NbU	1951+
DNLM	#	NcD	1+
DPU	1+	NcU	#
FMU	1+	NjP	1-9
FTaSU	1-[3] 4+	NmU	1+
GEU	1+	OCl	1-4
ICU	#	OU	#
IaAS	1951-55	PSt	#
KyU	#	TxU	1+
LU	1+	WU	1+
MH	1951-60	WaU	1+
MiU	1-8,10+		

9. <u>Boletim bibliográfico.</u> Biblioteca Pública Municipal. Sao Paulo, 1943-   a. (ir.)

"Contains sections, 'Colaboração original' and 'Autores e livros,' devoted respectively to articles on library techniques and to literary studies, usually reviewing a specific type of development, e.g., 'Alguns aspectos da poesia negra'. ...The [accession] lists continue to occupy the major portions of the 200 pages or more of each issue, but they are now nearly 10 years behind, and the gap is widening rapidly."

CLU	1-23	MoSW	3-23
CSt	1-23	MoU	3-23
CU	1+	NIC	1-23
CtY	1+	NN	1+
DLC	1-23	NNC	#
DPU	1+	NSyU	#
FMU	1-23	NcD	1-[2]+
FTaSU	1-23	NcU	#
FU	2-23	NjP	1-23

GEU	3-13, 15+	NmU	3-23
ICU	#	OrU	1950+
IU	3-23	PU	1+
IaU	1+	RPB	3-23
InNd	3,5, 9-10, 12,23	TNJ	4-6,9-23
		TxU	1-23
InU	22,23	UU	22-23
KU	22-23	ViU	3-23
KyU	#	WU	1+
LU	1-18,20+	WaU	1-13,15-23
MH	1-23		
MiDW	1-21		
MnU	3+		

10. Boletim carioca de geografia. Rio de Janeiro, 1950- q. ?
Associação dos Geógrafos Brasileiros. Seção Regional de
Rio de Janeiro.

"One of the more frequently cited of Brazil's regional
geographical journals."

CLU	#
CU	[1]+
IU	3-12
KyU	#
WU	[1]-[6]+

11. Boletim da Biblioteca da Câmara dos Deputados. Brasília,
1952-   s.a.

"Valuable for several reasons, particularly the 'Referencia
legislativa' section, which provides a semiannual index to
federal enactments under four main headings: (1) federal
laws, (2) legislative decrees, (3) resolutions of the Chamber of Deputies, (4) resolutions of the Senate. There is an
extensive bibliography on some timely topic, not necessar-
ily of exclusive or primary Brazilian interest..."

CLU	#	KU	10+
DLC	6+	KyU	#
DPU	1957+	MH	current issues
IU	[9-10]	NcU	#

12.   Boletim da Comissão Catarinense de Folclore.   Florianó-
       polis, Sta. Catarina, 1949-   ir.

       "Contains signed, well documented studies. Recent arrange-
       ment has been in three principal sections: state, national,
       and foreign. A Noticiário gives news of persons and events
       in Brazil and neighboring countries."

       CU   1+
       DLC   #
       TxU   no.2-4,6-8,
               17-24

13.   Boletim do Centro Latino-Americano de Pesquisas em
       Ciencias Sociais. Rio de Janeiro, 1958- bi-m. Title
       changed to America Latina with vol.5, 1962.

       "In addition to its informational function, the Boletim car-
       ries one or more signed articles, such as might be found
       in journals on the social and political sciences, and, in
       'Bibliografia,' books or articles on pertinent topics are
       reviewed."

CLU	4+	MH	1-4
CU	[1]+	MnU	1+
DCU	#	MoSW	4-5
DLC	[1-4]+	NN	2+
DPU	1+	TNJ	[2]+
FU	1+	TxU	[2-3]+
ICU	#	ViU	[2-4]
LNT	#	WU	4+

14.   Boletim do Instituto Joaquim Nabuco de Pesquisas Sociais.
       Recife, 1952-   a. At head of title: Ministério da Educa-
       ção e Cultura.

CU	1+	KyU	#
DCU	#	MH	1-9
DLC	1-9	NNC	#
DPU	1+	TxU	6
FU	6-9	ViU	2-3

15.   Boletim do Ministério do Trabalho, Indústria, e Comércio.
      Rio de Janeiro, 1934- Nova fase, 1951- q. Published
      by the Ministry's Serviço de Documentação.

      "New series contains much useful information, including a
      guide to relevant legislation, but has less textual material
      than formerly."

CSt	1-148,161-166	NN	1+
CU	125-166	NNC	#
CtY	105,112-130,	NcU	#
	133-134	NjP	[11]
DPU	1934+	NmU	#
FMU	#	TNJ	1-141,144,
KyU	#		146-148,161-166
MH	1940+	WU	4-12,22-43
MiU	4-15		45-166
MnU	[1937+]		

      Nova fase, 1951-   q.

CLU	1,3-[5]-7	MiU	1+
CSt	1951+	MnU	[1951+]
CU	1+	NN	1958
CtY	1+	NNC	#
DLC	1-9	NcD	1951+
DPU	1951+	NcU	#
FMU	#	NmU	#
FU	1-5	TNJ	1,4-9
IU	1951+	TxU	1[2],4-[10]
KyU	#	WU	1-5
MH	1951+		

16.   Boletim do Museu Nacional. Nova série: Antropologia.
      Rio de Janeiro, 1942- s.a.

      "Monographic studies by members of the Museum's staff.
      Range from 5 to 120 pages, including bibliographies."

CLU	1-15	N	1-19
CSt	1-5, 10+	NIC	#
CU	1+	NN	1-18
CtY	1-18,20	NNC	#
DLC	1-20	NbU	2-6
DPU	1+	NcD	1+
FMU	2+	NcU	#
FU	1-19	NmU	2+
ICU	#	OCl	#
IU	1-19	OrU	1943+
IaAS	#	PPiU	#
IaU	1-16,19	PU	1-10,13-19

InU	17-19	RPB	7-8,13-18
KU	1+	TNJ	6-7,9-11,
KyU	#		13-14,16,18
LNT	#	TxU	2-20
LU	2-18	ViU	2-19
MiDW	2-15	WU	2+
MiU	1+	WaU	#
MnU	1+		

17.   Boletim do Museu Paraense Emilio Goeldi. n. s.   Antropologia, Belem, Para, 1957- ir.   Conselho Nacional de
Pesquisas.   Instituto Nacional de Pesquisas da Amazônia.

"Issues contain a single contribution each, from an article
of a few pages to a monographic study of over 100."

CLU	#	LU	1+
CSt	1+	MiU	1+
CU	1-18	N	[2-5]
CtY	1+	NIC	1-15
DLC	1-10,12-17	NN	1+
DPU	1+	NNC	#
FU	1+	NmU	11+
ICU	#	PU	1+
IU	1-17	TxU	1-17
KU	1+	WU	1+

18.   Boletim geográfico.   Rio de Janeiro, 1943- bi-m.
Conselho Nacional de Geografia.   Supplements its Revista
brasileira de geografia.

"Contains an editorial, a section devoted to translations,
one containing brief 'contributions to scientific geography,'
news notes, chiefly from Brazil, the text of pertinent
legislation and 'Bibliografia e revista de revistas,' in
which one or more books and a half dozen issues of leading
geographical reviews are reviewed."

CLU	1-20	InU	1+
CSt	[2-13] 14+	KyU	#
CU	1+	LNT	#
CtY	[1]-[3]-[18]+	LU	1+
DCU	#	MH	1-19
DLC	1+	MnU	[1+]
DPU	1+	NNC	#
FMU	[1]+	NcU	#
FU	[1-3] 4+	NjP	14+
GEU	[1]-[3-4]-	NmU	[1-5],7+
	[7]-[9-10]	OU	#

ICU	#	PU	5+
IEN	1+	TNJ	1+
IU	1-20	TxU	1-20
IaU	14+	WU	1+

19. **Boletim informativo do IBBD.** Rio de Janeiro, 1955-
bi-m. (ir.) Instituto Brasileiro de Bibliografia e
Documentação.

"Its articles provide an informative account of professional
developments and technical guidance for Brazilian bibliog-
raphers. Its news notes cover a wide geographical range."

CLU	1-4	FU	1-4
CU	1+	KyU	#
DCU	#	N	1-4
DLC	1-4	NIC	1-4
DNLM	#	NNC	#
DPU	1+	NcU	#
FMU	1+	TxU	1-4

20. **Boletim paulista de geografia.** Sao Paulo, 1949- 3 times
a year. Associação dos Geógrafos Brasileiros. Seção
Regional de São Paulo.

"The 60 major studies presented had been distributed thus:
Geografia humana e econômica, 22; Geografia física e
Biogeografia, 9; Fotogeografia, 9; Estudos críticos e Notas
previas, 9; Metodologia e ensino da Geografia, 6; Antologia
geográfica, 5; Cartografia 1. In addition, reviews, bibliographies, and news..."

CLU	11-36	KyU	#
CSt	1+	MH	1-37
CU	1+	N	1-23
DCU	#	NIC	1-33
DLC	1-30,35,36,38	NN	1-30
DPU	1+	NNC	#
FMU	[1949]-53	NSyU	#
FU	1-2,4-15,23,34	NcD	1+
ICU	#	TxU	1-38
IU	1-28,31-38	WU	17-22,24+
InU	34+		

21.   <u>Brasil moderno</u>. Rio de Janeiro, 1951- q.

"'A quarterly magazine destined for showing the world
what Brazil is achieving in Engineering, Industry, Public
Works, Education, Banking and other fields.'
"The content is, accordingly, rather miscellaneous."

CU	#	MB	1955+
CtY	2-4,6+	MoSW	[3]
DPU	1+	NN	1-17
FU	8-14 [15] 16+	NcU	#
IU	[9]	TxU	1-[7],10-13
		ViU	9

22.   <u>Brazila esperantisto</u>. Rio de Janeiro, 1907- bi-m.

"They contain, besides one or more signed articles, original or in translation, chiefly news notes and a bibliographical section listing reviews or other publications from
throughout the world."

NN   1908,1911-12,
            [1915,1930]

23.   <u>Brazilian American survey</u>. Rio de Janeiro, 1953- q.

"Contains articles on history, culture, and economic and
social conditions in both countries in line with stated
objectives."

CLU	current issues	NNC	#
CSt	8+	NSyU	#
CU	8+	NcD	1957+
CtY	5+	NcU	#
DLC	[2-9]+	NjP	9-10,12-15
DPU	1955+	NmU	4-5,9,11-13
FU	8+	OCl	#
IU	1-3,6-19	OrU	1958+
KU	6+	PPiU	10+
MB	1958+	PSt	1958-59
MH	1-17	TxU	2,4-5,7-19
N	[7,10]	UU	1953+
NIC	7-17	ViU	4-9
NN	8+	WaU	11+

24.   Brazilian business. Rio de Janeiro, 1921-   m.

"Published jointly by the American Chambers of Commerce
for Brazil, it contains staff-written articles and sections,
notably 'Brazil at a glance' and 'Review of the exchange
situation.'"

CLU	#	N	2,3,9+
CU	39+	MH	#
CtY	[19-21]	NIC	[36] 37-41
DLC	1-26,28+	OCl	1922+
DPU	1946+	PU	5-13
ICU	#	ViU	12
LNT	#	TxU	[16-18]-[22-25],
			27 [28]-[36-37]-
			[39]+

25.   CAPES: boletim informativo da Campanha Nacional de
Aperfeiçoamento de Pessoal de Nível Superior. Rio de
Janeiro, 1952-   m.

"Current bulletins, of some 36 pages, are devoted primarily to staff written reports of events in Brazil's university
world and of other pertinent national and international
events, an opinion forum, in which newspaper or similar
comment is reproduced with a brief editorial note, relevant
official decrees, etc. Annual report in double issue during second quarter."

CU	1952+	FU	1960+
DLC	1952+	KyU	#
DPU	1952+	TxU	no.1-104

26.   Clã. Fortaleza, 1948-   ir.

"Clã illustrates the situation in which a regional literary
which proved successful gave rise to a publishing company."

DLC	1-11,15,16,18
DPU	1948+
NN	1,5-9,11
TxU	11-12

27.   Comércio internacional: boletim mensal do Banco do Brasil.
       Rio de Janeiro, 1951- m.

       "Contains chiefly repetitive statistical series covering the
       current year but may include special charts for longer
       periods."

CLU	1-11	NN	1-9
CU	current issues	NNC	#
CtY	[1]-[11]	NcU	#
DLC	1[2]3-9	NjP	1-9
DPU	1+	OCl	1+
FU	1-11	OrU	1+
ICU	#	RPB	1-11
IU	1-10	TNJ	[1]
KyU	#	TxU	1-[10]
MiU	1-4[5-6]7+	WU	1+
MoSW	1951-1955		

28.   Conjuntura econômica. International edition. Rio de
       Janeiro, 1954- m. Subtitle: Economics and business in
       Brazil.   Brazilian Institute of Economics. Getúlio
       Vargas Foundation. Center for Economic and Business
       Research.

       "International edition contains chiefly material translated
       from the parent one, less about Brazil. Sections vary
       somewhat, usually include a 'Special study' on some part
       of the world. Economic indexes, data on industry, finance,
       transportation, public service."

CLU	1-[8]	MiU	[1-2]3-7[8]+
CSt	1+	MnU	[1+]
CU	4-5,9+	MoSW	9+
CtY	1+	N	[1-6,8,9]
DLC	1-[17]+	NIC	1[2-4]-[6]-
DPU	1+		[8]-16
FMU	[1]-[3-4]+	NN	1-9
FU	1+	NNC	#
IEN	1+	NSyU	#
IU	4-9	NcU	#
InU	8+	NjP	1-8
KU	[1+]	OkU	2-11
LU	1+	OrU	1956+
MCM	1+	TxU	1+
MdBJ	#	WU	3+

29.   Correio do IBECC. Rio de Janeiro, 1958- q.   Instituto
      Brasileiro de Educação, Ciência e Cultura.

      "The bulletin, of some 24 pages, is important not only for
      its Brazilian news but also as a source of information about
      the work of Unesco in the western hemisphere."

      CLU   #
      CU   1+
      DLC   17
      DPU   1+
      FU   1-13

30.   O cruzeiro. Rio de Janeiro, 1928- w.

      "Illustrated news and general weekly magazine, one of the
      oldest and best of its kind in the Americas. Carries
      articles on events of international interest including special
      reports by its foreign correspondents, but it is particular-
      ly valuable as a record of social, economic, and cultural
      developments in Brazil and of Brazilian views on world
      affairs."

      CLU   32-36   DPU   1950+
      DLC   July 1939-   FU   [34] 35+
             Oct.1948,1949-   IU   [32-33] 34+
             1955,1956-June   MiU   current issues
             1959,Oct.-Nov.   MoU   1962+
             1961, [1963]   TxU   [20-21],Sept.1962+

31.   O cruzeiro internacional. Rio de Janeiro, 1957-
      fortnightly.

      "Contents are said to be selected from O cruzeiro and A
      cigarra and from material especially prepared for this
      edition. Similar in format to the parent publication, but
      less voluminous, due partially to the difference in advertis-
      ing carried."

      IU   3+

32.   Diálogo: revista de cultura. Sao Paulo, 1955- q.

      "Modern poetry, including translations, is a prominent fea-
      ture, often accompanied by critical commentary. Occasion-
      al articles deal with music or the plastic arts, others with
      such topics as historical perspective. 'Notas e resenhas'
      consists of brief articles and book reviews, signed by
      staff members. Books reviewed are chiefly in fields of the
      humanities, others in social sciences."

```
CU      1+
DPU     1955+
KyU     #
NN      9-11
```

33. Digesto econômico. Sao Paulo, 1944- bi-m. Subtitle:
     O mundo dos negócios num panorama mensal.

     "Digest format. Contains considerable reprint or trans-
     lated material, for which source is noted, but whether
     such articles are condensed is not stated. Some are as
     much as 20 pages in length and are apparently original.
     Most deal with some national or regional aspect of the
     Brazilian economy."

```
CLU     #
DLC     1-6,[8-9]-
        [13-16]+
NNC     #
TxU     no.50+
```

34. EBSA: documentário do ensino. Sao Paulo, 1947?- m.
     "'Orgão de informações e interêsse para o ensino médio.
     Publicação da Editora do Brasil, S/A.'"

     "A monthly bulletin devoted to the interests of secondary
     education in Brazil."

```
DLC     5-7 [8+]
FU      3,7,22-30,32-
        71,73-89,92-
        138,149
```

35. Econômica brasileira. Rio de Janeiro, 1955- q.
     "'Revista trimestral patrocinada pelo Clube de Economis-
     tas.'"

     "A compactly printed journal of 60 pages or more. In
     early issues, the two or three studies in each dealt chiefly
     with economic theory."

```
CSt     1963+           NIC     [2] 3-6
CU      2+              NN      1+
DLC     1-[8]           NNC     #
DPU     1955+           TxU     [2],5-8
IU      [4]             WU      [2]+
MnU     [5+]
```

36. Educação. Rio de Janeiro, 1940- q.   Associação
Brasileira de Educação.

"References in HLAS [Handbook of Latin American
Studies] note such items as a manifesto by the ABE in
defense of free public schools and the work being done by
various educational centers in Brazil."

CU	1-54
DLC	1-8,10-12, 21-53
DPU	1956+
PU	1-20
TxU	1-12

37. Educação e ciências sociais. Rio de Janeiro, 1956- q.
Centro Brasileiro de Pesquisas Educacionais

"Described in HLAS [Handbook of Latin American Studies]
(no.20,item 1798) as a quarterly bulletin whose objective
is the periodic reporting of the studies and social research
relating to education carried out by the Centro."

CU	9+	PPiU	9+
DLC	1-7	PSt	#
DPU	1+	TxU	no.2-3,6-8, 10-19
MH	no.1-2,16-19		
MoSW	1962+	WU	1962+
NjP	4-5		

38. Estudos sociais. Rio de Janeiro, 1958- bi-m.

"Opening editorial (maio-junho 1958) stated that Estudos
sociais was a review of Marxist tendencies. As such it
would seek to participate in discussion of questions related
to Brazil's economic, social, and political problems and
also in developments looking towards national emancipa-
tion.... Carries substantial, documented articles along
lines indicated."

CLU	#
DLC	[1958-59]
DPU	1959+
NNC	#

39.   Folclore. Vitória, Espírito Santo, 1949- ir. Comissão
      Espírito-Santense de Folclore.

      "Currently a small bulletin of irregular appearance, but
      useful as a source of information about folklore organiza-
      tions in Brazil and their work."

CLU	no.1-63
DLC	no.55-74
KyU	#
NN	no.61-69

40.   Habitat: arquitetura e artes no Brasil. Sao Paulo,
      1950- bi-m.

      "A handsome review, covering not only all phases of Bra-
      zilian art, including popular and primitive, as well as
      architecture, but various art manifestations in other coun-
      tries and continents."

CLU	#	LU	4+
CSt	1,[12-31],67	MCM	23,26,28-29
CU	1+	MH	2+
CtY	#	MnU	4+
DLC	3-51,67,69-70	NIC	67+
DPU	1+	NN	3,5,7-10,
FMU	[2],[5-6]+		12-14,16-45
FU	8+	NNC	#
IU	1-15,17-18,20,	OkU	2-62
	22-25,27-32,	PU	1+
	34-36,38-39,43+	TxU	43-70
InNd	1958-61	UU	64,66+

41.   IDORT: revista de organização e produtividade. Sao Paulo,
      1932- m.   Formerly: Revista de organização científica.
      "'Instituto de Organização Racional do Trabalho, comité
      nacional brasileiro, filiado ao Comité Internacional de
      l'Organization Scientifique (CIOS).'"

      "Contains, in addition to official reports, editorials and
      original articles having to do with labor problems, rela-
      tions with commerce and industry, personnel studies, etc."

CLU	#
DLC	13+
DPU	1941+
NN	no.1-3,5-170,
	172-191,193-
	254
NNC	#

42. Industriários. Rio de Janeiro, 1948- bi-m.
"'Orgão oficial do I.A.P. (Instituto de Aposentadoria e
Pensões dos Industriários).'"

"Contents include articles and news concerning social security in Brazil and occasionally regarding other countries
or international aspects. Authors are usually identified
by position held. Finances receive considerable attention,
but as much as three-fourths of the publication is devoted to
legal matters. Charts, tables."

CLU	#
DLC	no. 1-89
DPU	1952+
NN	no.49-69
TxU	no.1-20,22-86

43. Jornal de letras. Rio de Janeiro, 1949- m.

"Contains articles on literary or cultural themes, chiefly
by well-known Brazilian writers, and numerous brief
articles or comments. Has sections on the plastic arts and
cinema, sometimes one on music, a 'panorama do mundo,'
and usually sections on cultural events in other parts of
Brazil and Portugal."

CU	1949-55	MH	1949-56
DLC	1-6,14+	NN	1949-57
DPU	1950+	NcU	#
ICMILC	1956+	PSt	#
IU	no.7-91,93,	PU	1951-55 (film)
	97-107,109-119,	TxU	no.1-14,16-81,
	124, 130-135,		83-97,99-100,
	137-141,143-150,		163+
	153+		

44. Kriterion: revista da Faculdade de Filosofia da Universidade de Minas Gerais. Belo Horizonte, 1947- q. (s.a.)

"Contains articles, or sections of longer studies, on philosophy, language and literature, and, to a lesser extent, on
the exact or social sciences. Authors are chiefly professors
at the sponsoring or neighboring universities. Kriterion
is an important source of up-to-date information about
scholarly works, especially in the humanities and social
sciences, published in Brazil, including translations."

CLU	[3],5-13	LU	11+
CSt	1-6,13-18	MH	5-14
CU	8+	MdBJ	#
CtY	5+	MiU	no.33+
DCU	#	NIC	[8],10-11,13+
DLC	7-13	NN	7-13
DPU	1952+	NNC	#
FMU	[5],7-10+	NcU	#
FU	[1],4-14	NjP	no.35-40,43-54
IEN	6-10	TxU	6-14
InNd	5-7	ViU	8-13
InU	#	WU	[8]+
KyU	#		
LNT	#		

45.   Manchete. Rio de Janeiro, 1952- w.

"Illustrated general and news magazine. Popular style,
staff-written, with numerous photographs."

CLU	1952+
DPU	no.4+
FU	no.[38-536]+
TxU	no.541+

46.   MEC (Ministério de Educação e Cultura). Rio de Janeiro,
1956- ir.

"Includes articles and speeches by Brazilian or other
functionaries, news notes, and a 'Registro bibliográfico'
of publications received."

DLC	1-5
DPU	1956+
IEN	11+
KyU	#
MH	1-4

47.   Mensagem econômica. Belo Horizonte, 1952- m.
"'Orgão oficial da Associação Comercial de Minas Gerais
e da Federação das Associações Comercias de Minas
Gerais.'"

"A bulletin of some 40 pages containing editorials, articles,
news of business and commerce and of the Association.
Some articles are substantial and of considerable extent...."

CLU	#
DPU	1952+

48.   Módulo: revista de arquitetura e artes plásticas.   Rio de
Janeiro, 1955-   q. ?

"Shows evidence of high professional standards and awareness of the relationship between the plastic arts, architectural form, and city planning on the one hand and the
social, cultural, and economic problems of the country on
the other.   The articles, plans, photographs, art reproductions, and maps deal mainly with Brazilian topics...."

CSt	2+	NIC	no.21+
CU	1+	NN	no.5+
CtU	3+	NNC	#
CtY	#	NSyU	#
DLC	3+	NcU	#
DPU	1957+	NmU	7+
FMU	no.7+	OkU	6-18
FU	no.7,15,17+	PSt	#
GAT	1+	TxU	no.7+
IU	no.1,3+	ViU	[2],3-5
LNT	#	UU	no.7,9-15,
LU	no.18+		17-20,22-31
MdBJ	#		
MoSW	2+		

49.   Mundo melhor. Sao Paulo, 1958- m. Subtitle: Diretrizes
e experiências humanas.

"A family magazine, one which, according to editorial
statements, attempts to give its readers a Christian and
modern view of the world, of man and his problems, and
frequently to offer solutions to those problems, whether
individual, social, political, economic, or moral. Somewhat similar to the Reader's Digest in appearance and
type of contents, it contains original materials by Brazilian
writers, mainly essays and comments on movies, art, and
current events."

DPU   1958+

50.   Música sacra. Petrópolis, 1940- bi-m.

"Contains original articles, translations, and news notes
dealing with the history, criticism, techniques of sacred
music and with musicians. Some music."

DLC	1-17
DPU	1949-54
IU	80-86
UU	#

51.   O observador econômico e financeiro. Rio de Janeiro,
       1936- m.

"Contains one or more signed feature articles, often profusely illustrated, and several shorter staff-written ones,
besides regular sections on various phases of the economic
life of Brazil. Considerable attention is given to power
development, industries, commerce, basic agricultural
produces and problems, special features relating to various
states or regions, and occasionally to neighboring countries
or matters of international interest."

CLU	1946-61	IU	10-27
CSt	[2]-11	MH	#
CU	18,88-203,209+	MiU	12-40
CtY	3,9-23,29-[30-	MoSW	#
	39]	NN	17-25
DLC	1-22,24,27	NNC	#
DPU	1936+	OU	#
FU	169-192,203-	TNJ	1+
	206,208-243,	TxU	159-174,176-
	245-246,248-		193,195+
	250,253-254,		
	257,259		

52.   A ordem: orgão de centro Dom Vital. Rio de Janeiro,
       1921- m.

"'A strongly Catholic journal which publishes a small
number of serious philosophical, biographical, and critical
articles by outstanding Catholic thinkers of Brazil and
Europe.'"

DCU	#	TxU	[46-47]-[50-
DLC	39-53,55-61		55]-[58-60]-
DPU	1934+		[65-66]
NcD	20,22-[24]-		
	[55]-[59]+		

53.   Revista brasileira de economia. Rio de Janeiro, 1947- q.
       Published by the Fundação Getúlio Vargas under the
       direction of the Instituto Brasileiro de Economia.

"Established to provide for independent research, for
teaching economic theory, and for the promoting of a
better understanding of the possibilities of applied economics with regard to Brazil. Contains up to six original
articles or studies, including series of classroom lectures
by visiting professors, tending heavily towards economic
theory."

CLU	2-15	MCM	[16]
CSt	1-9	MH	1-15
CU	1+	MiU	[1]-3
CtY	1-14,16+	MoSW	#
DLC	1-16	NIC	1,[2-4],5+
DPU	1+	NNC	#
FMU	1+	NSyU	#
FU	1-9,[15]+	NcD	1+
IEN	1+	NjP	1-[9]
IU	[15]	PU	1-11
InU	#	TNJ	1-14
KU	3-[7],9-10,	TxU	1+
	13+	ViU	[4]
MB	6+	WU	3-13

54.   Revista brasileira de estatística.   Rio de Janeiro, 1940-
q. (s.a.)
"'Orgão oficial do Conselho Nacional de Estatística da
Sociedade Brasileira de Estatística, editado trimestral-
mente pelo Instituto Brasileiro de Geografia e Estatística.'"

"Important technical journal, useful for Brazilian studies
and to some extent for those of other American countries.
Cited less frequently than formerly because of the decrease
in textual material.... Contents tend towards technical
topics, such as methodology and vocabulary, but usually
include articles on specific problems, notably demography."

CLU	1-19	MiU	1[3]+
CSt	1+	MnU	[1+]
CU	1+	NIC	1+
CtY	1+	NN	1-21
DCU	#	NNC	#
DLC	1+	NSyU	#
DNLM	#	NcD	1-[2-4]+
DPU	1+	NcU	#
FMU	[1]-[3-6]+	NjP	[1-10]
FU	[1-3],6+	NmU	[1-2],[8]+
ICU	#	OU	#
IEN	1+	OkU	8-21
IU	20+	OrU	#
IaAS	6+	PPiU	1-2
IaU	1-2,5,7+	PU	1+
InNd	[1]	RBP	#
InU	1,9,11-13,	TNJ	1-3,6-23
	15-20	TxU	no.1-10,13-15,
KU	61+		18-20,22-25,27,
KyU	#		29-91/92
LNT	#	ViU	1-2-[3]-22
LU	1-8 [9-28]+	UU	1-2
MH	1-22	WU	1-[3-4]+
MdBJ	#		
MiDW	1-16		

55. Revista brasileira de estudos pedagógicos. Rio de Janeiro,
     1944-   q.   Ministério de Educação e Cultura. Instituto
     Nacional de Estudos Pedagógicos.

"Aim, restated in each issue, is to expound and discuss
general pedagogic questions, especially those of Brazil,
to provide facts, and to attempt to reflect the thinking of
its teachers. It hopes to contribute to advanced standards
of public opinion regarding education."

CLU	1-[7-8]-9,	MiU	[1]+
	33-36	N	1-17,20
CU	1+	NN	[1-3]
CtY	1-4,10-26	NNC	#
	[27-30]+	NcU	#
DLC	1+	NmU	32-33,39-42,
DPU	1+		46-48
FU	7-20,25-70,	PU	12-30,32+
	72+	TxU	1+
KyU	#		

56. Revista brasileira de estudos políticos. Belo Horizonte,
     1956-   s.a.   Universidade de Minas Gerais. Conselho
     Universitário.

"Contains ten or more substantial articles on political
theory and practice and closely related topics. The few by
non-Brazilians are chiefly translations from U.S. and
other sources."

CLU	6-14	MiU	1+
CSt	1+	MoSU	2-12
CU	1+	N	5-8,17
DCU	#	NIC	[1]-3, 8+
DLC	1-[3-4]+	NNC	#
DPU	1958+	NSyU	#
FU	1+	NjP	1,8-13
InNd	1-3,7-12	NmU	[1]+
KU	13+	PU	1+
LNT	#	TxU	1+
MH	1-15	ViU	2-3,8,10-14
MdU	1962+	WU	2+

57.   Revista brasileira de filosofia. Sao Paulo, 1951-   q.
      "'Orgão oficial do Instituto Brasileiro de Filosofia.'"

      "The articles, which include lectures and conference
      papers, show an awareness of man's need for a philosophi-
      cal approach to questions of art, music, language, histori-
      cal knowledge, economic systems, and to human relations
      in the new space age. There are usually two or three arti-
      cles on controversial topics in a section called 'Temas em
      debate.'"

CU	1+	NN	1-23
DLC	1+	NNC	#
DPU	1951+	NcU	#
IU	10-12	PSt	1955+
KyU	#	TxU	27,29,31,
MH	[1-11]		33-34,37
MoSU	7-12		

58.   Revista brasileira de geografia. Rio de Janeiro, 1939-   q.
      "'Orgão do Conselho Nacional de Geografia.'"

      "A review of high professional caliber. Studies presented
      are usually by persons connected with the CNG or the parent
      Instituto Brasileiro de Geografia e Estatística (IBGE)....
      Typical subject headings from annual index show varied as-
      pects of geography treated: biological, economic, physical,
      historical, human (including demography), political,
      regional and urban, and methodology."

CLU	1-[8]+	MnU	[1+]
CSt	1+	NIC	19+
CU	1+	NN	1-23
CtY	1+	NNC	#
DCU	#	NSyU	#
DLC	11+	NcD	[1]+
DPU	1+	NjP	1-4,9-11,17,
FMU	1+		19-21,23
FU	[1]+	NmU	[1-8]+
GEU	[4-5]-[7-8]-	OCl	#
	[11-14]	OU	#
IEN	1+	OkU	1-15,17,18,
IU	21+		20,21
IaU	1+	PPiU	[2,3,5,7]
InNd	2-15	PSt	1950+
InU	2+	PU	1+
KU	19-21	RPB	[2-3],5[6]-[8]
KyU	#		-[16-17]-21
LNT	#	TNJ	1-23
LU	1+	TU	10+
MCM	1-[3]-[6-8]-	TxU	1+
	21	ViU	2

MH	1-22	UU	[2]
MdBJ	#	WU	1+
MnU	[1+]	WaU	[1]-[3-4,6,
MiU	1+		19]

59.   Revista brasileira de política internacional. Rio de Janeiro, 1958-   q.   Instituto Brasileiro de Relações Inter-
nacionais.

"Usual issue contains six or seven articles, chiefly by
Brazilian diplomats, economists, or professors. Topics
treated fall into three main groups: international questions
of general importance, problems which concern Latin
America as a whole, and considerations of the position of
Brazil or some other country with regard to a specific
situation."

CLU	1+	MoSU	3+
CSt	1+	MoU	1+
CU	1+	NIC	1+
CtY	1+	NN	2+
DCU	#	NNC	#
DLC	1-4	NjP	1-2
DPU	1+	NmU	1+
FMU	1+	OU	#
FTaSu	1+	OkU	current issues
FU	1+	OrU	1+
ICU	#	PSt	#
IaU	1+	PU	1+
InNd	1+	RPB	1-4
InU	1+	TU	1+
KU	1+	TxU	1+
KyU	#	ViU	1-3
LNT	#	UU	1-5
MH	1-18	WU	1+
MiU	2+	WaU	1-4

60.   Revista brasileira dos municípios. Rio de Janeiro, 1948-
q.   Sponsored by: Conselho Nacional de Estatística and
Associação Brasileira dos Municípios.

"Contains articles on city and regional planning or problems,
especially as they pertain to Brazil. Some reprints from
sources such as the OAS. Economic, social, and legal aspects are treated. Contains also news, reports on legislation and judicial decisions, demographic data, etc."

Cty	#	NIC	7-14
DLC	2-16	NN	no.17-38
DPU	1+	NSyU	#
FMU	[5-6]	TNJ	1-12,14-15
InU	13+	TxU	no.6-14,35-36
MH	[no.19-52]	ViU	[1]

61.   Revista brasiliense. Sao Paulo, 1955- bi-m.

"The 200 pages or so of a bimonthly issue usually contain
an editorial and some 15 articles, largely in social science
fields but with some literary criticism."

CLU	1+	NIC	27+
CU	1+	NN	1-38
DLC	1-5,7+	NNC	#
DPU	1+	TxU	1-5,7+
FU	34+	WU	1-4,7+
MH	1-39	WaU	1961+

62.   Revista da Academia Paulista de Letras. Sao Paulo,
       1937?-   ir.

"...a typical academy bulletin, publishing studies in
language and literature, bio-bibliographies of members,
and miscellaneous notes."

CLU	1-[15]-21	DPU	1938+
CSt	1-15	KyU	#
CU	1+	MH	1958-62
CtY	3-15	MiU	14,19,30,31,
DLC	[1-2,6-9,		41,43-44
	12-22]	NcU	#
		NjP	19-20

63.   Revista da Campanha Nacional de Educação Rural. Rio de
       Janeiro, 1954-   ir. (a. or s.a.)   Published by the
       Campanha Nacional de Educação Rural (CNER).   At the
       head of title: Ministério de Educação e Cultura.

"The Revista contains reports on research studies by the
CNER, with commentary, accounts of its official activities,
including participation in congresses, news notes, etc.
Issue for first half of 1959 was a monographic history of
the CNER from planning stage in 1950 to date."

DPU	1954-58
FU	1-8
KyU	#

64.   <u>Revista da semana</u>. Rio de Janeiro, 1889-   w.

"...'primarily a profusely illustrated news journal' but in
addition stresses the artistic photographs and popular art
features."

DLC   [40-54]
DPU   1950+
NN   1953-58

65.   <u>Revista da Sociedade Brasileira de Geografia</u>. Rio de
Janeiro, 1885-   a.(ir.) Formerly: <u>Revista da
Sociedade Brasileira de Geografia do Rio de Janeiro</u>.

"It continues to carry, in addition to accounts of Society
business, 'serious articles relating to all parts of Brazil,
geographical and anthropological in character', and 'some
biographical sketches.'"

CLU	8-12,14,18-30,	FMU	19-28,30-34,
	37-42,44-48,		37,39,49-55
	50-52,54-55	KyU	#
CSt	1-9,29,31,35-	MH	1-55
	54	MiU	1-48,52
CU	1+	NN	1-[37-38]-55
CtY	#	TxU	1-10,18-33,
DLC	1-33,35-55		35,37-53
DPU	1923+		

66.   <u>Revista da Universidade Católica de Campinas</u>. Campinas,
1954-   ir.

"General university review containing chiefly articles in
fields of philosophy, religion, medicine, and law, by university professors. Occasional articles on important social
aspects of Brazilian culture or international relations."

DLC   1-3
KyU   #
NN   6+

67.   <u>Revista da Universidade Católica de Sao Paulo</u>. Sao Paulo,
1952-   q.

"A general university review.... Of the six to eight articles
or lectures, usually at least one is specifically relevant to
Brazilian culture."

DLC	1+	NN	1-16
DPU	1+	TxU	no.8-11,13-
FU	38		14,16-17,
KyU	#		20-30,34+
MH	1-9		

68.   Revista de administração municipal. Rio de Janeiro,
       1954-   bi-m.   Formerly Notícias municipais (1954-
       1960).

       "The considerable number of articles, studies, decisions
       of the Supreme Court, book notes, and other writings which
       had appeared during the eight years of the periodical's
       existence were considered to make of it the most valuable
       collection of materials on municipal administration and
       planning yet published in Brazil."

       CLU   current issues
       DLC   3+
       DPU   1+
       FU   1+

69.   Revista de antropologia. Sao Paulo, 1953-   s.a.
       "'Orgão oficial da Associação Brasileira de Antropologia
       e da Sociedade Brasileira de Sociologia.'"

       "Concerned primarily with social rather than physical
       anthropology. Most of the several articles deal with
       specifically Brazilian topics, but some are on theory, re-
       lationships between anthropology and other fields, or
       cultures of neighboring countries or continents."

CLU	1+	NN	1+
CU	1+	NNC	#
DLC	1-5,7-8	NcD	2+
DPU	1+	NmU	1+
FU	1+	PPiU	5+
ICU	#	PU	1+
IU	1+	TU	8+
InU	1+	TxU	4[5]-7
KyU	#	WU	1+
MH	1+	WaU	1-7
MoU	1962+		

70.   Revista de finanças publicas. Rio de Janeiro, 1941-   bi-m.
       Ministério de Fazenda. Conselho Técnico de Economia e
       Finanças.

       "Often reviewed in Notícias municipais, according to which
       it has sections on various phases of public finance."

       CU   22+
       CtY   #
       DLC   [12-20],22+
       DPU   1952+
       MoSW   no.15-18

71.   <u>Revista de história</u>. Sao Paulo, 1950-   q.
       "'Orgão do Departamento de História da Faculdade de
       Filosofia, Ciências e Letras da Universidade de São Paulo.'"

"Successes of the first decade, as noted in anniversary
editorial, included prestige gained by the quality of its
articles, most of which dealt with Brazilian history, and
the providing of a link between the university faculty and
history teachers throughout Brazil. A plea was made to
professors in the interior of the country to whom primary
sources were available to seek them out and contribute
them. Contributors are chiefly Brazilian professors, but
articles by U.S. or other authors also occur."

CLU	1-5,7-25	NNC	#
CSt	1+	NSyU	#
CU	1+	NcD	1+
CtY	1+	NcU	#
DCU	#	NjP	no.4,6-13,
DLC	1,3-4,12-13,16+		16,18-48
DPU	1+	NmU	1+
FU	1+	OkU	1-10,12-16,
ICU	#		18-21
IU	3-4,9,14-15,22	PSt	#
KyU	#	PU	1+
MH	1-12	RPB	1-16,19-21,23
MiU	no.1-26,28+	TNJ	1-3,6-9,13-21
MnU	4+	TxU	1+
MoSU	no.37-49	WU	no.1-14,20,
N	1-2,13-15,17,		23, 25+
	22+		
NN	1+		

72.   <u>Revista do Arquivo Municipal</u>. Sao Paulo, 1934-   q.(ir.)
       "Publicação da Divisão do Arquivo Histórico, do Departa-
       mento de Cultura, da Secretaria de Educação e Cultura da
       Prefeitura de São Paulo.'"

"In the mid-1950's several issues were devoted to historical documents and current legislation, but in general the
contents have been articles or extensive studies in the
fields of the social sciences and the humanities, preponder-
antly cultural history and folklore. The subject is usually
local or national, but it may range afield, with its claim to
a place in the Sao Paulo archive the fact that a lecture was
delivered there."

CLU	1,6-11,17-18,	NIC	81-154,156,158+
	20-27,29-35,37-	NN	1
	134,136-166	NNC	#
CSt	[1-19]	NSyU	#
CU	1+	NcD	1-164
CtY	[1-95],97+	NjP	1-65,67-81,
DCU	#		83-156,162-164
DLC	81,83-93,97-108,	NmU	[1-2,4]-[7] 8
	110-154,158+	PSt	#
DPU	1+	PU	1-39,41-154
FMU	6+	RPB	13,16-20,22-30,
FU	50-62,64-81,83-		32-38
	101,103-106,108,	TxU	6,9,21-22,29-30
	112-115,134-135,		32-34,37-38,40-41,
	141-143,145,148-		43,46-166
	156	UU	[1-162]
IEN	[1934-1950],150+	WU	38-81,83+
KyU	#	WaU	78-81,83-94,
LNT	#		96-109,124,
LU	1-151,162		127-143,145-146
MH	[1-27]		
MiU	7-11,21-34,42-		
	154,156,158+		

73. **Revista do Conselho Nacional de Economia.** Rio de Janeiro, 1952-   bi-m.

"Contains extensively documented articles, lectures, and reports on economic matters of concern to Brazil, including general Latin American topics."

CU	8+	MH	[1952-59]
DLC	1-11	NN	1+
DPU	1953+	NNC	#
FU	[7]+	OrU	#
IU	3-10	TxU	5-[8]+
KyU	#		

74. **Revista do ensino.** Porto Alegre, 1951-   8 nos. a year.
"'Publicação da Secretaria de Educação e Cultura do Rio Grande do Sul.'"

"A general educational review with emphasis on materials and methods for the elementary school."

CLU	#	DPU	1953+
CU	#	FU	8+
DLC	no.17-51,55+	MoSU	no.75-79,82-89

75.   Revista do I. R. B. (Instituto de Resseguros do Brasil).
       Rio de Janeiro, 1940-   bi-m.

       "Contains articles and studies on technical matters,
       national and international problems and developments,
       statistics, etc. Sections include ones on news, legislation
       or decisions, and a 'Boletim do I. R. B.'"

DLC	[1-6]+	MH	5+
DPU	1947+	TxU	[1952]
KyU	#		

76.   Revista do Instituto Brasil-Estados Unidos. Rio de Janeiro,
       1943-   a.

       "Content centers on single theme, e.g., literature, tech-
       nical problems, economic cooperation."

CLU	1-15	MiU	[1]-14
CU	1+	NN	1,10,13
CtY	1-17,20	NNC	#
DLC	1-13	NcD	1-11
DPU	1+	NcU	#
FMU	1-3,[5]-7	NjP	1-10,13-15
FU	12-15	PU	1-7
ICU	#	TNJ	[1+]
LNT	#	TxU	1-11
MH	1943-59	WU	1+

77.   Revista do Instituto de Geografia e História Militar do
       Brasil. Rio de Janeiro, 1941-   ir. (a. or s.a.)

       "Contains articles and discourses by members of the
       Institute, which by a decree of November 28,1949, was
       recognized as an official consultative organ. Biographical
       materials may be the most useful feature of this review."

CU	1+
DLC	1-4
FU	21,23
KyU	#

78.   Revista do Instituto Histórico e Geográfico Brasileiro.
       Rio de Janeiro, 1839-   q.

"Qualitatively, it is widely credited with having set high
standards for social science research in Brazil.
"Geographical studies are of relatively less importance than
in earlier years. The same is true for folklore, ethno-
graphy, and other fields than history, both as to contributions of members and as to 'documentos,' of which, for
instance, a series in t. 78, 1915, was devoted to plastic
arts in Brazil. Scope is not limited exclusively to Brazil.
A member may contribute a study of some outstanding
figure in a neighboring country, possibly with a somewhat
remote Brazilian connection."

CLU	1-10,12-[26,	MiU	1-166,170-
	28,30],31,34-		241,245+
	[37,38]-[41]-51,	MnU	1-108
	53-68-[69,70]-	N	1-47,178-190,
	[73]-[76]-78,		192-195,201-202,
	80-81,83-85,		214-243
	87-88,90-109,	NN	203-246
	164-244,247+	NNC	#
CSt	1+	NNH	1+
CU	1+	NcD	1-73,75-109,
CtY	1-166,179+		164+
DCU	#	NjP	1-166,179+
DLC	1-58,69,[72]76,	NmU	4,[5],139,172,
	[79] 80-109,164-		183
	166,170,178+	OCl	1+
DPU	1+	OU	#
FMU	1-11,14-35,38-	PU	1-6,8-13,15-22,
	[48],50-[59-60],		24-25,27-31,34-
	66-74,78-79,82-		84,139-167,172,
	83,86-92,109-		178-243
	116,119-120,125,	TNJ	1939+
	141-147,149-	TxU	1+
	154,156-166,	ViU	8,30',108
	179-181,183-	WU	1+
	188,190,192		
FU	1-87,91,97,108,		
	165-187,189-		
	221,230+		
ICN	1+		
ICU	#		
InU	1962+		
KyU	#		
MH	1-250		

79.   Revista do Instituto Histórico e Geográfico de São Paulo.
       Sao Paulo, 1895-   ir.

       "Contents of issues examined are more properly history,
       anthropology, and folklore than history and geography.
       Contributions include valuable studies in the three fields
       and collections of documents on various aspects of the
       Brazilian past."

CSt	1-16,19-27, 32	MiU	1-36
CU	1+	NN	1-58
CtY	1-27	NNC	#
DCU	#	NcD	1+
DLC	1-27,37-59	NcU	#
DPU	1948+	NmU	4,14,20,39-52
FU	56-58		
ICN	1+	TNJ	1+
KyU	#	TxU	53-59
MH	[1-40]		

80.   Revista do livro. Rio de Janeiro, 1956-   q.
       "'Orgão do Instituto Nacional do Livro, Ministério da
       Educação e Cultura.'"

       "The usual issue contains ten or more studies, dealing
       chiefly with Brazilian or Portuguese writers and literature,
       brief sections devoted to unpublished literary documents
       and to reprints, and several other sections among and
       within which arrangement varies somewhat. 'Noticiário'
       provides a list of the publications of the I. N. L. including
       this Revista (with full table of contents for the preceding
       issue), and it may contain, for instance, a summary of the
       literary events of the year."

CLU	1-2,10-24	KU	23-24
CU	1+	KyU	#
CtY	14,16-17,19-20	MH	1-6
DLC	1-6	MiU	1+
DPU	1959-60	NIC	no.17-24
FMU	[2]	NNC	#
FU	[1-2]3-5	NcU	#
IEN	1+	OrU	5+
IU	1-6	TxU	1-20,23-26
InU	2+	WU	1+

81.   Revista do Museu Júlio de Castilhos e Arquivo Histórico
      do Rio Grande do Sul. Porto Alegre, 1952-   a.   At
      head of title: Secretaria de Educação e Cultura.

      "Contains studies, reprinted materials, and documents
      concerning colonization, genealogy, natural history, in-
      digenous peoples, gauchos, and their traditions, etc."

CLU	#	FMU	1+
CU	#	KyU	#
DCU	#	TxU	1-6
DLC	1-7	WU	1+
DPU	1+		

82.   Revista do Museu Paulista. Sao Paulo, nova série, 1947-
      q.

      "Subject matter is South American Indians, principally
      those of Brazil. Scholarly studies, chiefly social anthro-
      pology, occasionally sociology or history. Ethnology
      section made a special report in 1952."

CLU	1-12	MdBJ	#
CU	1+	N	#
CtY	1+	NIC	1-12
DCU	#	NNC	#
DLC	1-12	NcD	1-12
DNLM	#	NjP	1-4
DPU	1+	NmU	1-6,9+
FU	3-12	PU	1-12
ICU	#	PPiU	9-10
KyU	#	TxU	1-12
LU	1-7,9+	UU	2-4
MH	1-10	WU	1-6
MiU	1-10	WaU	2,4-8

83.   Revista do Patrimônio Histórico e Artístico Nacional. Rio
      de Janeiro, 1937-   ir. Ministério de Educação e Cultura.

      "Deals with historical places and buildings, architectural
      features, colonial and 19th century painting, etc. Some
      biography. Extensive documentation."

CSt	2,11,13-14	MoSU	11-14
CU	2-13	NIC	1-4,12-14
CtY	1-14	NNC	1+
DCU	#	NNH	3,6-14
DLC	1+	NcD	2-4, 6+
DPU	1945+	NjP	2-14
FU	9-14	NmU	14
KyU	#	PU	1-4,6-9,11-14
MiU	2-14	TxU	1-14
MnU	8-14		

84. **Revista do professor.** Sao Paulo, 1941?-   m.
Centro do Professorado Paulista.

"Articles relating efforts on behalf of rural education in
Bahia were cited in HLAS [Handbook of Latin American
Studies] no.21, item 1761."

DLC   not retained

85. **Revista do Serviço Público.** Rio de Janeiro, 1937-   m.
Brazil. Departamento Administrativo do Serviço Público.

"Concerned with governmental organization and procedure
at all levels, also with personnel and organization problems
of public service institutions. Contributions are signed,
mostly original but some translations."

CLU	[1]-[9]-10,[12] -[14,15]-[17-19] -[21]	MiU	1-29,59-67,72, 74-77,83,86-88, 92+
CSt	3+	MnU	[4+]
CU	[1]	MoSW	1963+
CtY	[1-2]-[8-11]+	MoU	[74]+
DCU	#	N	66-[74]-[78] -[83]+
DLC	ano 1-10[11-16] no.83+	NIC	1-14
DNLM	#	NN	1-23
DPU	1+	NNC	#
FMU	[1940-44]-[1948], [1950],[1956]	NSyU	#
FU	[1,4-5]+	NbU	84+
GEU	[8-10],12-[13] -[15]-[18-19]+	NcD	[1]-[3]+
		NcU	#
ICU	#	NmU	[8-11]-[15]- [17]-[23]+
IEN	1+		
IU	[1938-39]+	OU	#
InU	[8-10]+	OkU	71-75,77-87
KU	1-77	Oru	1950+

KyU	#	PPiU	1945+
LNT	#	PU	1-18,20+
MH	1-88	RPB	8
MdBJ	#	TxU	1-94(some issues
MdU	1952+		wanting)
MiDW	8,11+	WU	[1]-[4,5]-
			[8-11]+
		WaU	[2-3],[9+]

86. Revista do trabalho. Rio de Janeiro, 1933-   bi-m.
Sociedade Editora Revista do Trabalho, Ltda.

"Average issue of some 50 pages contains a brief editorial,
two articles, four sections on legal aspects of labor matters. Important on this basis and as a non-governmental
publication in the field."

CLU	#	DPU	1934+
DLC	11-15,18-19,	ICMILC	#
	21-27		
DNLM	#		

87. Revista Esso. Rio de Janeiro, 1945-   q.
"'Uma publicação trimestral da Esso Standard do Brasil,
Inc.'"

"Somewhat less deluxe than its Venezuelan counterpart,
but typical issue contains three well illustrated, staff-
written articles on art and a variety of others of social
science interest, most of which are not directly connected
with the oil industry."

DPU	1954+
TxU	1955-1962

88. Revista geográfica. (PAIGH) Rio de Janeiro, 1941- s.a.
Instituto Pan-Americano de Geografia e História. Com-
missão de Geografia.

"May feature a lengthy report, but usually contains articles
in Portuguese, Spanish, or English on topics of general
interest or of concern to an area. News notes from various
countries of the Americas and Europe. Obituaries are
bio-bibliographical. Bibliographical features irregular,
but often important."

CSt	[1]-4	LU	1-16
CU	#	MdBJ	#
DLC	1+	MoSU	[25]
DPU	#	MoU	1941-1957
FMU	1-8,13-14,23,	NNC	#
	25-30	NmU	1-4
FTaSU	[2]+	OCl	#
FU	1+	PU	1-8,26-27
ICU	#	TU	22+
IaU	3-4,9-17	TxU	1-30
InU	1-4,9+	WU	1+
KyU	#		
LNT	#		

89.   Revista interamericana do ministério público.   Sao Paulo,
      1956-   ir.

"Contents are largely legal in nature, but some of the
original studies and reprints are of interest historically
or to the political or social scientist.   Most articles are in
Portuguese, a few in Spanish and/or English."

DLC	1-4	NN	1+
DPU	1+	NNC	#
FU	1-3	TxU	1,3-4
MH	1+		

90.   Revista marítima brasileira.   Rio de Janeiro, 1881-   q.
      Ministerio da Marinha

"Contains articles, addresses, documents, about Brazilian
naval history and information on technical developments
in Brazil or elsewhere.   Obituary notices, with minimum
data."

CLU	71-78	MdBJ	#
CSt	57+	NN	17-81
CtY	[17-18,34,42,	NNC	#
	47],52-[61]-	NcD	[39],[60-62]-
	[64]-[69]-[72-74]		[69-70]-[72-74]
DLC	17-25,27-35,	PU	[52]-79
	51+	TxU	[69]-72,
FU	72+		[77]-79
KyU	#		
MH	[1898-1920,		
	1932-61]		

91. Seleções do Reader's Digest. Rio de Janeiro, 1942-   m.
     Subtitle: Condensações de artigos de interêsse permanente.

     "Publication authorized by the Reader's Digest Association,
     Inc."

CtY	1-[17]-19	NmU	current issues
DLC	1-24	OrU	1948+
FTaSU	current issues	TxU	1-[2]
FU	13-29	ViU	[3]
IU	11-15		

92. Sintese política econômica social. Rio de Janeiro, 1959-
     q. Subtitle: Orgão oficial do Instituto de Estudos Políti-
     cos e Sociais da Pontifícia Universidade Católica do Rio
     de Janeiro.

     "Contains an editorial, three or more articles by members
     of an extensive panel of contributors, and sections devoted
     to 'syntheses' of the events of the quarter in each of the
     three fields indicated, under their respective section edit-
     ors. 'Livros e revistas' contains signed reviews of a
     number of Brazilian and other new, relevant titles and a
     classified list of additional books received, with full
     bibliographical data."

CLU	current issues	InNd	current issues
CSt	1+	MH	1-4
CU	1+	MoSW	1963+
CtY	3-4,6-9,11-14	NN	1+
DLC	1+	NNC	#
DPU	1+	TxU	2-8,10-13

93. Sociologia. Sao Paulo, 1939-   q.
     Subtitle: Revista dedicada à teoria e pesquisas nas
     ciências sociais. Escola de Sociologia e Política, Institu-
     ção Complementar da Universidade de São Paulo.

     "As the first Brazilian journal in its field, it was meant to
     provide a compendium of materials for sociology students
     more flexible than books could provide, to encourage the
     undertaking of field studies, the direct observation and
     study of concrete facts in order to provide the fundament-
     als for sound study of the social realities of Brazil...
     "The same types of materials continue to predominate,
     but some articles now deal with developments in other
     countries or areas or those of inter-American interest.
     Articles,in English and translations occasionally appear."

CLU	[1]-24	MoSU	1-8,19-24
CSt	11+	MoSW	15+
CU	[11]+	NN	[1]-18
CtY	[11]	NNC	#
DLC	1+	NcD	1+
DPU	1+	NcU	#
FU	[3-6]-[8-10]+	NjP	[12-17]
IEN	[5]+	OrU	1958
IU	6-24	TNJ	22
IaU	23+	TU	22+
InU	6-17,19+	TxU	[1]-[11]+
LU	[3-14]+	WU	25+
MH	3-24		

94. Subsídios para a história maritima do Brasil. Rio de
     Janeiro, 1938- ir.(a.) Ministério da Marinha. Serviço
     de Documentação Geral da Marinha.

     "Contains documents, articles, chronologies, etc. of
     interest for the maritime history of Brazil."

CLU	#	FU	12-16
CSt	1-4,6-16	KyU	#
CU	1+	MH	1-14,17-18
DLC	7-16	TxU	1-12

95. Verbum. Rio de Janeiro, 1944-   q.   Pontifícia Univer-
     sidade Católica do Rio de Janeiro.

     "Devoted largely to doctrine and religious history, or to
     religious aspects of current events or problems. Occas-
     ional articles on legal, ethnological, or sociological topics.
     Brief bio-bibliographies of authors. Usual sections:
     Notas y comentários, Resenha de livros, Resenha de re-
     vistas, and Livros recebidos."

CLU	1	InNd	2-18
CU	1+	KyU	#
DCU	#	MH	[8]-13
DLC	7+	MoSU	13-[19]
DPU	1949+	NN	9-18
FU	[3,6,8],9,13	NNC	#
IU	[16,17]	TxU	[1-3],6-19

96. Veritas. Porto Alegre, Brasil, 1955-   q.   Subtitle:
Revista da Pontifícia Universidade Católica do Rio Grande
do Sul.

"One of the more frequently cited of Brazilian university
reviews. Indexing provided by the Bibliografia brasileira
de educação and the CML [Columbus Memorial Library,
Pan American Union] List shows it to be a source of information regarding the thinking of outstanding Brazilians
over a period of time. Contains other studies of humanities
interest, e.g., on philology."

CLU	1-7	MH	1-7
CU	1+	NN	1-6
DLC	1,3-4,6+	TxU	18+
DPU	1957+		

97. Visão. Rio de Janeiro, 1952-   w.

"Portuguese edition of Visión. Has addresses also in Sao
Paulo and Porto Alegre."

CLU	#	FU	21+
CSt	[4],6+	InU	22+
CU	13+	MoSW	19+
DLC	4+	NIC	1963+

98. Vozes: revista católica de cultura. Petrópolis, 1907-   m.

"Addressed to the Catholic intellectual, aims primarily to
provide present day orientation. Contains a half dozen
original articles, mainly on current topics but some with
historical interest, a similar section of shorter signed
items, 'Ideas e fatos,' and a dozen signed reviews of recent books, including translations; chiefly Brazilian publications."

CLU	current issues	MoSU	56 [57]
DLC	1-36,n.s.1-14,	NN	53-56
	51-[54],57+	TxU	1943-1953,
DPU	1945+		[1962]
FU	[36,48-54]		

BRAZILIAN
HISTORY

F 2501   Periodicals. Societies. Collections*
              Collected works
  2502   Several authors
  2503   Individual authors
                 Including collected papers, addresses, essays
                     etc.
    .5   Museums. Exhibitions, exhibits
  2504   Gazetteers. Dictionaries. Geographic names
    .5   Directories
           Biography
  2505   Collective
               Individual, see F 2520.6, 2524-2651
  2508   General works
    .5   Juvenile works
  2509   Minor works. Pamphlets addresses essays, etc.
    .3   Anecdotes, legends, pageants, etc.
                Cf. GR 133, Folklore
                     PN, PQ, etc., Literature
    .5   Guidebooks. Handbooks
    .7   Historic monuments (General)
  2510   Social life and customs. Civilization. Intellectual life
               Including national characteristics. Race con-
               flicts and problems, see F 2659

           Description and travel. Views
  2511   Early to 1821
  2513   1822-1889
  2515   1890-1950
  2516   1951-

---

*U. S. Library of Congress, Subject Cataloging Division, *Classification. History; Class E-F: America* (3d ed.; Washington [U. S. Govt. Print. Off.] 1958). Changes and additions taken from official copy in Subject Cataloging Division, July 1964.

                    Antiquities. Indians
F 2519   General works
      .1   Local (Ancient and modern), A-Z
                    .A6   Amazon Valley
                    .B3   Bahia (State)
                    .G68 Goyaz (State)
                    .L3   Lagoa Santa
                    .M4   Matto Grosso (State)
                    .P2   Pará (State)
                    .P8   Purus River
                    .R5   Rio de Janeiro (State)
                    .R6   Rio Grande do Sul (State)
                    .S2   São Paulo (State)
      .3   Topics (Ancient and modern), A-Z
                    .A7   Art
                    .B6   Bows and arrows
                    .C3   Cannibalism
                    .D2   Dances
                    .E2   Education
                    .F6   Feather work
                    *P6   Pottery
                    .R3   Religion. Mythology
                    .S6   Social life and customs
                    .W7   Writing
      2520   Modern Indians (General)
      .1   Tribes (Ancient and modern), A-Z
                          Amahuaca, see F 3430.1.A5
                    .A6   Apalai
                    .A63 Apalakiri
                    .A64 Apiacá
                    .A65 Apinagé
                    .A7   Arara
                    .A75 Araua
                          Arawak, see F 2230.2.A7
                          Arecuna, see F 2380.1.A7
                    .B3   Bakairi
                    .B4   Baré
                          Betoya, see F 2270.2.B4
                          Boro, see F 2270.2.B6
                    .B75 Bororo
                    .B76 Botocudo
                    .C3   Cadioeo
                          Caingua, see F 2230.2.C3
                    .C32 Canella
                    .C35 Caraja
                          Carib, see F 2001
                    .C37 Caripuna

Antiquities. Indians
F 2520.1   Tribes (Ancient and modern), A-Z--Continued
    .C4   Catoquina
    .C45   Cayapo
          Chamacoco, <u>see</u> F 3320.2.C5
          Chapacura, <u>see</u> F 3320.2.C375
          Charrua, <u>see</u> F 2719.2.C5
    .C5   Chavante
    .C6   Chipaya
          Chiquito, <u>see</u> F 3320.2.C3
    .C7   Crichana
    .F8   Fulnio
    .G6   Goyataca
    .G7   Guajajara
    .G73   Guana
          Guarani, <u>see</u> F 2230.2.G72
          Guayana, <u>see</u> F 2230.2.G75
          Guayaqui, <u>see</u> F 2679.2.G9
          Guaycuru, <u>see</u> F 2230.2.G78
    .I6   Ipurucotó
    .J8   Juruna
    .K3   Kaingangue
    .K35   Kamaiurá
    .K4   Kariri
    .K5   Kashinaua
    .M2   Macu
          Macusi, <u>see</u> F 2380.1.M3
    .M3   Maue
          Mayoruna, <u>see</u> F 3430.1.M45
          Mbaya, <u>see</u> F 2679.2.M3
          Moxo, <u>see</u> F 3319
    .M8   Mundurucu
    .M9   Mura
    .N3   Nambicuara
          Omagua, <u>see</u> F 3430.1.O5
          Oyampi, <u>see</u> F 2460.1.O9
          Oyana, <u>see</u> F 2230.2.O8
          Pacaguara, <u>see</u> F 3320.2.P3
    .P3   Painguá
          Pano, <u>see</u> F 3430.1.P3
    .P4   Parentintin
    .P45   Pauishana
          Peban, <u>see</u> F 3430.1.P4
          Piro, <u>see</u> F 3430.1.P5
    ..P8   Puri
    .S3   Sanavirona
    .T3   Tapuya

                      Antiquities. Indians
F 2520.1   Tribes (Ancient and modern), A-Z--Continued
                      .T4   Tenetehara
                      .T45   Tereno
                      .T5   Timbira
                             Trio, see F 2420.1.T7
                      .T7   Trumai
                      .T9   Tucano
                      .T925 Tucuna
                             Tupi, see F 2230.2.T84
                      .T94   Tupinamba
                      .U3   Uaboi
                      .U5   Umotina
                      .U7   Urubu
                             Wapisiana, see F 2380.1.W3

                History
        .3   Chronological tables, Outlines, syllabi, etc.
                      Questions and answers, etc.
                  Historiography
        .4   General works
                      Biography of historians
        .5   Collective
        .6   Individual, A-Z
                              e.g. .A2 Abreu, João Capistrano de
                                    .P4 Pereira da Costa, Francisco
                                         Augusto
        .7   Study and teaching
      2521   General works
                      Including political history
                  General special
      2522   Military and naval history
                      Diplomatic history. Foreign and general rela-
                          lations
      2523   General works
        .5   Relations with individual countries, A-Z
                            For List of countries in one alphabet,
                                see p. 472-473
                        United States, see E 183.8.B7
        .9   Other (not A-Z)
                  By period.
                      Pre-Columbian period, see F 2519-2520.1
      2524   1500-1821
      2526   1500-1548
                          Discovery, exploration, and coloniza-
                              tion by Portuguese
                          Cf. E 123, Demarkation Line of Alex-
                              ander VI

History
By period
F 2528   1549-1762
Bandeiras (General; if limited to a
state, class with state); expulsion of
Jesuits, 1760; etc.
Biography: José de Anchieta (Cf. BX
4705.A57, Catholic Church); Salva-
dor Correia de Sá e Benavides; Mem
de Sá; Antônio Vieira (Cf. BX 4705.
V55, Catholic Church); etc.
Cf. F 2684, Jesuit missions of Paraguay,
War of the Seven Reductions
(Guarani War), 1754-1756
F 2723, Portuguese settlement at
Colonia, Uruguay
2529   French colony at Rio de Janeiro, 1555-
1567
Biography: Nicolas Durand de Villega-
gnon, etc.
2530   Spanish control, 1580-1640
2532   Dutch conquest, 1624-1654
Capture of Bahia, 1625; battles at
Guararapes, 1648 and 1649; capture
of Olinda, 1630; etc.
Biography: Henrique Dias, João Fer-
nandes Vieira, etc.
2534   1763-1821
Portuguese court in Brazil, 1808-1821;
revolt in Pernambuco, 1817; etc.
Biography: Joaquim José da Silva Xavier,
etc.
Cf. DP 650, João VI, king of Portugal
F 2461, French Guiana
F 2723, Expulsion of Brazilians from
Colonia
2535   1822--
2536   Empire, 1822-1889
Pedro I, 1822-1831; Regency, 1831-1841;
Pedro II, 1841-1889
Brazil declared independent of Portugal
on September 7, 1822; Empire estab-
lished on October 12, 1822; Revolution
of 1842; separatist movement in Rio
Grande do Sul, 1845; etc.

History
By period
1822--

F 2536   Empire, 1822-1889--Continued
Biography: José Bonifacio de Andrada e
Silva (Cf. PQ 9697. A74, as author);
Benjamin Constant Botelho de Maga-
lhães; Luiz Alves de Lima e Silva, du-
que de Caxias; Marcilio Dias; Diogo
Antonio Feijo; Giuseppe Garibaldi(Cf.
DG 552. 8. G2, as Italian patriot); Irineo
Evangelista de Souza, visconde de
Maua; Joaquim Nabuco; Joaquim Mar-
ques Lisbôa, marques de Tamandare;
etc.
Cf. F 2687, Paraguayan War, 1865-1870
F 2725, War with Argentina over
Uruguay, 1825-1828
F 2846. 3, War with Argentina, 1849-
1852
2537   Republic, 1889--
Including special period, 1889-1930
Brazil declared a republic, November 15,
1889
Naval revolt of 1893-1894; Conselheiro
Insurrection, 1897; military revolution
of 1924-1925, etc.
Biography: Ruy Barbosa; Manuel Ferraz
de Campos Salles; Manuel Deodoro da
Fonseca; Antonio Vicente Mendes Maciel;
Manuel de Oliveira Lima; Floriano
Peixoto; José Gomes Pinheiro Machado;
José Maria da Silva Paranhos, barão
do Rio Branco; etc.
Cf. D 501-680, World War I, 1914-1918
2538   1930-1954. Period of Vargas
Revolution of 1930; Communist Revolution
of 1935; Integralist Revolt of 1938, etc.
Biography: Eurico Gaspar Dutra, Getúlio
Vargas, etc.
Cf. D 731-838, World War II, 1939-1945
.2   1954-

Regions, states, etc.
2540   Acre (Territory)
Cf. F 2546, Amazonas boundary
2541   Alagoas

                    Regions, states, etc. --Continued
F 2543   Amapá (Territory)
   2546   Amazonas
                        Amazon River and Valley; Içá River; Japurá
                            (Yapurá) River; Javarí (Yavarí) River; Jurua
                            River; Jutaí (Jutahy) River; Purus River;
                            Rio Negro; etc.
                        Cf. F 2281.A4, Amazon River and Valley,
                            Colombia
                            F3451.A4, Amazonas (Peru)
                            F3451.L8, Amazon River and Valley, Peru
   2551   Bahia (Baía)
                        Cf. F 2601, Pernambuco boundary
                            F 2636, Sergipe boundary
   2554   Boundaries
                        .A1-8   General
                        .A82   Argentina
                                    Misiones question, see F 2916
                        .B6   Bolivia
                                    Cf. F 2540, Acre (Territory)
                        .B8   British Guiana
                        .C7   Colombia
                        .D8   Dutch Guiana, Surinam
                        .F8   French Guiana
                        .P3   Paraguay
                        .P4   Peru
                        .U8   Uruguay
                        .V4   Venezuela
   2556   Ceará
   2558   Counani
                        Contested territory awarded to Brazil
                    Distrito Federal, see F 2646 and 2647
   2561   Espírito Santo
                        Colonies of Germans, Poles, Swedes, Tyro-
                            lese, etc.
   2564   Fernando de Noronha Island (Territory)
   2566   Goyaz (Goiás, Goiaz)
                        Araguaya River, Tocantins River, etc.
   2567   Guanabara
                    Guaporé (Territory), see Rondônia (Territory)
   2568   Marajó (Island)
                        French Colony, 1612-1618
   2571   Maranhão
                        Gurupy River, Parnahyba (Parnaíba) River,
                            etc.

Regions, states, etc. --Continued
F 2576   Matto Grosso (Mato Grosso)
                        Araguaya River, Garças River, Xingú
                            River, etc.
                        Cf. F 2566, Goyaz boundary
                            F 2684, Jesuit missions of Paraguay
      2581   Minas Geraes (Minas Gerais)
                        Mucury Colony, etc.
      2586   Pará
                        Rivers: Araguaya, Capim, Gurupy (Gurupi),
                            Tapajos, Tocantins, Parú, Xingú, etc.
                        Marajó Island, see F 2586
                        Cf. F 2546, Amazonas boundary.
      2591   Parahyba (Paraíba)
      2596   Paraná
                        Assunguy Colony, Guayra Falls, Iguazú
                            River and Falls, (Cf. F 2909, Argentina),
                            Paraná River, etc.
                        Cf. F 2684, Jesuit missions of Paraguay
      2601   Pernambuco
      2606   Piauhy (Piauí)
                        Parnahyba (Parnaíba) River, etc.
                        Cf. F 2571, Maranhão Boundary
      2609   Rio Branco (Territory)
      2611   Rio de Janeiro (State)
                        Parahyba (Paraíba) do Sul River and Valley,
                            etc.
                        Rio de Janeiro (Federal District and City),
                            see F 2646
      2616   Rio Grande do Norte
                        Cf. F 2556, Ceará boundary
      2621   Rio Grande do Sul
                        German colonies; Revolution of the Farrapos,
                            1835-1845; etc.
                        Gauchos, Brazilian (Cf. F 2217, General)
                        Cf. F 2684, Jesuit missions; War of the
                            Seven Reductions, 1754-1756
      2624   Rondônia (Territory)
      2626   Santa Catharina (Santa Catarina)
                        Part of Misiones awarded to Brazil. Cf. F
                            2916, Misiones Territory of Argentina
                        German colonies, e.g. Blumenau; Itajahy
                            (Itajaí) River and Valley; etc.
                        Cf. F 2596, Paraná boundary
                            F 2916, Misiones award (General)
      2629   São Francisco River and Valley

Regions, states, etc. --Continued
F 2631   São Paulo
                        Bandeiras; Revolution of 1932; etc. Rivers:
                            Aguapehy (Aguapeí) Juquiá, Paraná,
                            Peixe, Ribeira de Iguape, Tieté; etc.
                        Cf. F 2581, Minas Geraes boundary
                            F 2684, Jesuit missions of Paraguay;
                            War of the Seven Reductions, 1754

    2636   Sergipe

                Cities, towns, etc., A-Z
    2646   Rio de Janeiro (City; and Federal District until
                    April 21, 1960)
    2647   Brasília (City; and Federal District, April 21,
                    1960-)
    2651   Other, A-Z
                        e.g.   Bahia, see .S13, Salvador
                        .B4   Belém
                        .B42   Belo Horizonte
                        .C83   Curitiba
                        .F6   Fontaleza
                        .N5   Niteroi (Nictheroy)
                        .O9   Ouro Preto
                        .P15   Palmares
                                 Pará, see .B4, Belem
                                 Pernambuco, see .R4, Recife
                        .P8   Porto Alegre
                        .R4   Recife
                        .S13   Salvador
                        .S15   Santos
                        .S2   São Paulo

    2659   Elements in the population
                    For interpretation, see F 1392
                .A1   General works
                            Including foreign elements (General)
                                minorities, race conflicts and prob-
                                lems, etc.
                .A2-Z Individual elements
                        e.g.   .A5   Americans
                               .B4   Belgians
                               .B7   British
                               .E8   Estonians
                               .F8   French
                               .G3   Germans
                                     Indians, see F 2519-2520.1

F 2659   Elements in the population
                    .A2-Z   Individual elements -- Continued
                            .I8   Italians
                            .J3   Japanese
                            .J5   Jews
                            .N4   Negroes
                                          Cf. HT 1126-1130,
                                              Slavery
                            .P8   Portuguese

LIBRARY OF CONGRESS CLASSIFICATION:

BRAZILIAN LITERATURE

		History and criticism*
		Periodicals, Societies, Collections, etc.
PQ	9500	Periodicals
	9501	Yearbooks
	9502	Societies
	9503	Congresses
		Collections
	9504	Series. Monographs by different authors
		Collected works, studies, essays of individual authors
	9506	Encyclopedias. Dictionaries
		Study and teaching
	9508	General
	9509	Schools
	9509.5	Biography of scholars, teachers, etc., A-Z
		Authorship, see PN
		History
		General
	9510	Early works
	9511	Modern treatises
	9512	Compends. Text-books
	9513	Outlines, Syllabi, Quizzes, etc.
	9514	Collected essays
	9516	Lectures, addresses, pamphlets
		General Special
	9518	Relations to history, civilization, culture, etc.
	9519	Relations to other literatures
	9520	Translations
		Treatment of special subjects, classes, etc.
	9522	Subjects, A-Z
		e.g. Nature, Religion

* U. S. Library of Congress, Subject Cataloging Division, *Classification. Class P, Subclass PQ, Part 2: Italian, Spanish, and Portuguese Literatures, with Supplementary Pages* (Washington [U. S. Govt. Print. Off.] 1955). Changes and additions taken from official copy in Subject Cataloging Division, July 1964.

History and criticism --Continued
    History
        General special

PQ 9523   Classes, A-Z
               e.g. Jews, Priests
        Biography

9527   Collected
          By period, see special period below
          Individual, see 9696-9698.36

9529   Memoirs, letters, etc.
9531   Literary landmarks. Homes and haunts of authors
9533   Women authors. Literary relations of women
        By period

9535   Origins
9538-40   Medieval
9541-43   Modern. General   Under each:
9544-46   Renaissance   (1) Treatises. Compends
9547-49   16th-18th century (2) Collected essays
9550-52   19th century   (3) Special subjects
9553-55   20th century
    Poetry
        History

9561   General
9563   Medieval, see 9538-9540
9565   Modern. General
9567   16th-18th centuries
9569   (18th and) 19th century
9571   20th century
        Special

9577   Epic
9579   Lyric
9580   Popular poetry. Ballads, etc.
9581   Other, A-Z
    Drama
        History

9583   General
9585   Early
9587   19th century
9589   20th century
9593   Special forms, A-Z
9595   Special subjects, A-Z
    Prose. Fiction
        History

9597   General
9599   Early to 1800

                    History and criticism--Continued
                        Prose. Fiction
                            History
PQ 9601   19th century
    9603   20th century
    9607   Special topics, A-Z
                        Other forms
    9609   Oratory
    9611   Letters
    9613   Essays
    9615   Wit and humor
    9617   Miscellaneous
    9621   Folk literature
    .Z5   Minor works. Essays, pamphlets, etc.
                    Collections
                        General
    9631   Early to 1800
    9633   Modern
    9635   Minor. Selections. Anthologies
    9637   Translations, by language, A-Z
                        By period
    9640   Medieval
    9641   16th-18th centuries
    9643   19th century
    9644   20th century
    9647   Local, see 9546, 9594-9595, 9691-9692
                    Poetry
                        General collections
    9649   Early to 1800
    9650   Modern
    9651   Minor. Selections. Anthologies
    9653   Women poets
                        By period
    9655   Medieval
    9656   15th-18th centuries
    9657   19th century
    9658   20th century
                        Special. By form or subject, A-Z
    9660   Popular poetry, Ballads, etc.
                                    Cf. 9689
    9661   Other, A-Z
                                    e.g. .L8 Lyrics, Songs
    9663   Translations
                    Drama
    9664   General
    9665   Minor

Collections--Continued
Drama
By period

PQ 9666	To 1800	
9667	19th century	
9669	20th century	
9670	Special (Tragedies, Comedies, etc.), A-Z	

Prose
General

9672	Early to 1800	
9673	Modern	

Fiction

9675	General	
9676	Minor	
9679	Oratory	
9681	Letters	
9683	Essays	
9685	Wit and Humor	
9687	Miscellany	
9689	Folk literature	
	Cf. 9660	
9691	Special regions, provinces, etc., A-Z	
	e.g.	.M3-32	Matto Grosso
		.M3	History
		.M32	Collections
		.M32A1-19	Periodicals and Societies
		.M5	Minas Geraes
		.P4	Pernambuco
		.R5	Rio Grande do Sul
		.S3-4	Sao Paulo
		.S3	History
		.S4	Collections
9692	By place, A-Z	
	e.g. B3-4 Bahia	
9693	Foreign countries, A-Z	
9696	Individual authors to 1800, A-Z	
9697	Individual authors, 19th-20th century, A-Z	
.A53	Alencar, José Martiniano de, 1829-1877	
.A58	Almeida, Guilherme de	

PQ 9697	Individual authors, 19th-20th century, A-Z -- Continued
.A93	Azevedo, Aluizio, 1858-1913
.A95	Azevedo, Arthur, 1855-1908
.B37	Barroso, Gustavo, 1888-
.B55	Bilac, Olavo dos Guimarães, 1865-1918
.C35	Castro Alves, Antonio de, 1847-1871
.C42	Coelho Netto, Henrique, 1864-1934
.C75	Cruls, Gastão
.E7	Escragnolle Taunay, Alfredo de, 1843-1899
.F8264	Freire, Luiz José Junqueira, 1832-1855
.G75	Gonçalvez Dias, Antonio, 1823-1864
.G8	Graça Aranha, José Pereira da, 1868-1931
.G9	Guimarães, Bernardo, 1825-1884
.L59	Lobato, José Bento Monteiro, 1883-1948
.L74	Lopes de Almeida, Julia, 1862-1934
.M15	Macedo, Joaquim Manuel de, 1820-1882
.M18	Machado de Assis, Joaquim Maria, 1839-1908
.M225	Magalhães, Valentim, 1859-1903
.M35	Medeiros e Albuquerque, José Joaquim de Campos da Costa, 1867-1934
.M48	Menotti del Picchia, Paulo, 1892-
.O5	Oliveira, Alberto de, 1859-1937
.P35	Peixoto, Afranio, 1876-1947
.P6	Pires, Cornelio
.T43	Teixeira, Mucio Scœvola Lopes, 1857-1926

9698-9698.36	Individual authors, 1961- , A-Z
	Here are usually to be classified authors beginning to publish about 1950, flourishing after 1960.
	The author number is determined by the second letter of the name
9698	Anonymous
.1	A
.12	B
.13	C
.14	D
.15	E
.16	F
.17	G
.18	H
.19	I
.2	J
.21	K
.22	L

PQ 9698-9698.36 Individual authors, 1961--, A-Z --Continued

.23	M
.24	N
.25	O
.26	P
.27	Q
.28	R
.29	S
.3	T
.31	U
.32	V
.33	W
.34	X
.35	Y
.36	Z

9699   Translations, by language, A-Z
                  e.g. .F7 French

BRAZIL IN THE
LIBRARY OF CONGRESS CLASSIFICATION:
A SELECTIVE INDEX

INTRODUCTORY NOTE

The purpose of this index is to provide the user with the class numbers in the Library of Congress Classification for materials on Brazil. While there is general awareness of the fact that this scheme contains many numbers for topics treated in relation to countries, this index brings together for the first time such references for a specific country. At first glance this might appear to be a simple task, even though no general index to the Classification exists. (But even if it did, one doubts that it would list, under each country, all topics for which geographic subdivision is applicable.) Cumulating the indexes to the individual classes does not, however, accomplish this, because a majority of them contain no entries at all under Brazil. Therefore, the only way to determine the locations of materials for Brazilian studies is to review the schedules, page by page. Provision for Brazil, usually accomplished by means of references to supplementary tables, sometimes takes the form of a single number, under which the nations of the world or of South America are arranged alphabetically with symbols designating and differentiating them. In the latter instance B7 generally represents Brazil, but this symbol is constant only within a single class. Checking the analysis of the schedules against the shelf list at the Library of Congress before compiling the index provided an opportunity to verify all numbers actually in use (hence the variation in symbols for Brazil: each one appearing here corresponds to one or more entries in the shelf list.) However, there are also listings for which no books are yet present in the Library of Congress collections. This index, while extensive, does not pretend to contain every number in the Classification which might be utilized for Brazilian materials.

Every class contributed at least several entries, but it was necessary to establish some general policies for inclusion. Since the extensive portions of Classes F and PQ dealing with Brazil are reproduced completely as Appendices 3 and 4, not all possible topics from these classes received listing, nor was it practical to include personal names. In general, Brazilian cities and states are found only when referring to classes other than F and PQ, but historical events (wars, revolutions, and the like) and names of rivers do receive listing.

Careful study of the list of Library of Congress subject headings and of the "Relativ Index" of the Decimal Classification helped to determine the form of this index. Although obviously differing from both, it more nearly parallels the latter than the former. However, terms from the classification schedules were checked against the subject heading list, and whereʹver possible the same forms of entry are utilized. There are, in addition, entries under synonymous terms (many of them suggested by "see" references). Phrases consisting of two nouns connected by "and" receive entry under each; similarly those consisting of a noun and modifying adjective appear once in their normal order and again in their inverted form. On the other hand, form divisions (e.g., study and teaching, documents) are used as subdivisions under subjects; duplicate entry under the form does not seem justified. Exception was made in several cases, however-- most importantly for "Laws and Legislation," because it shows the dispersion of legal material on special topics through the Classification. (Class K, when published, will presumably provide for all legal material.)

Since all entries in this index relate to Brazil, the entry words assume that relationship and begin with the significant subject word (e.g., "Revolution of 1930," not "Brazil--History-- Revolution of 1930" or "Brazilian Revolution of 1930"), except in those few cases where the nationality word is essential to the meaning. Each listing gives the class number for the subject, but, in cases where a block of numbers is available (e.g., "Banking   HG 2881-2890"), the reader would need to consult the schedules for subdivisions of the topic and the corresponding numbers.

This index, containing approximately 700 entries (exclusive of subdivisions), should facilitate the location of material on specific topics in libraries or bibliographies arranged by the Library of Congress Classification.

Japanese Element in the Population	F 2659.J3
Japurá River	F 2546
Jesuits	
Expulsion	F 2528
Religious Orders	BX 2566-2567
Jewelry	NK 7333
Journalism	PN 5021-5030
Judaism	BM 266-267
Judicial Power	JL 2470
Juquiá River	F 2631
Jurua River	F 2546
Jutaí River	F 2546
Juvenile Literature	PZ 81-87
History	F 2508.5
Kindergarten	LB 1295-1297
Knighthood and Chivalry	CR 6277
Labor	HD 8281-8290
Classes	HD 6022-6025
Hours	HD 5152-5155
Social Conditions	HD 7023
Labor and the State	HD 7862-7865
Labor Disputes	HD 5352-5355
Labor Exchanges	HD 5902-5905
Labor Laws and Legislation	HD 7862-7865
Labor Market	HD 5752-5755
Labor Supply	HD 5752-5755
Labor Unions	HD 6611-6615
Lace and Lace Making	NK 9433
Land	HD 491-500
Land Tax	HJ 4319-4321
Landmarks, Literary	PQ 9531
Languages, Indian	PM 5151-5154
Laws and Legislation	
Accounting	HF 5620.B7
Advertising	HF 5819.B7
Aeronautics	HE 9925.B7
Commercial	HF 1302-1305
Engineering	TA 241-242
Fish and Game	SK 485
Forests and Forestry	SD 581-582
International	JX 4335.B8
Labor	HD 7862-7865
Military	UB 540-544

Municipal Ownership	HD 4632-4635
Mural Painting and Decoration	ND 2698
Museums	AM 34. B7
History	F 2503.5
Music	
Literature	ML 232
Songs	M 1689-1690
Nationality	
Vital Statistics	HB 3073
Natural History	
Geographical Distribution	QH 117
Naval Architecture	VM 41-42
Study and Teaching	VM 191-192
Naval Art and Science	VB 41-42
Naval Education	V 472-474
Naval Maintenance	VC 119-122
Naval History	F 2522
Naval Law	VB 450-459
Naval Medicine	VG 141-142
Naval Ordnance	VF 41-42
Naval Revolt, 1893-1894	F 2537
Naval Seamen	VD 41-42
Drill Regulations	VD 182-184
Naval Surgery	RD 241
Navigation (Aeronautics)	TL 525. B8
Navigation, Inland	HE 653
Navy	VA 422-424
Needlework	NK 9133
Needlework and Textile Arts	NK 8833
Newspapers	
Advertising	
Guides	HF 5963
History	HF 6105. B7
Nobility (Titles)	CR 3790
Normal Schools	LB 2041-2042
Numismatics	CJ 2260-2279
Occupations	
Vital Statistics	HB 2653
Official Documents	J 207-208
Official Gazette	J 6. B8-9
Omnibuses	HE 5653
Oratory	
History	PQ 9609
Orders of Knighthood and Chivalry	CR 6277

Societies

General	AS	80
History	F	2501
Literature	PQ	9500
Sociology	HS	2362-2365

Sociology

History	HM	22.B8

Songs

National	M	1689-1690
Popular	M	1690.2

Spanish Control, 1580-1640	F	2530
Spectacles	PN	3215.B7
Speculation	HG	5331-5340
Sports	GV	597-598
Stage	PN	2470-2474
Stage Lines	HE	5653
Stained Glass	NK	5333
Stamp Tax	HJ	5396
Standard of Living	HD	7023
State and Art	N	8965
State and Labor	HD	7862-7865
State Industries	HD	4091-4095
State Medicine	RA	207-208
State Ownership	HD	4091-4095

States

Constitutions	JL	2499
Government	JS	2423
History	F	2540-2636
Literature	PQ	9691
Maps	G	5410-5663

Statistics

Age	HB	1603
Births	HB	973
Census	HA	971-980
Classes	HB	2863
Deaths	HB	1393
Domicile	HB	2023
Rural	HB	2443
Urban	HB	2233
Libraries	Z	907
Marriages	HB	1183
Nationality	HB	3073
Professions	HB	2653
Sex	HB	1813

Street Railroads

Economics	HE	4621-4630
Technology	TF	741-742

Index of Libraries

This index does not include any references to the Bibliography or to the Appendices.

WITHDRAWAL